THANK You !

Robert C Pram
Last Chance, ID
Sept 18, 1996
Railroad Ranch
Steve, Chuck.

PASSION
BELOW ZERO

Essays from Last Chance, Idaho

DAVID HAYS

Helen Thompson
A-Bar

Editors: Debra Kronenberg and Dan Casali
Book and cover design by Dan Casali
Cover photo by David Hays
Author photo by Robert Bower

ISBN 1-885719-01-9
Published by   Lost River Press
                  P.O. Box 1286
                  Ketchum, Idaho 83340
                  (208) 726-5120

Printed by Publisher's Press
Salt Lake City, Utah, USA

10 9 8 7 6 5 4 3 2 1

Table of Contents

Introduction vii

1989
A New Beginning 1
Growing Old Gracefully 3
Home 5

1990
The Dreaded Cabin Fever 9
The Poet Who Died of Spring 13
Trout Connection 16
Tom 19
Splendor in the Grass .23
Pulling the Plug 26
A Crevice in Time 29
The Gift is in the Giving 32
An Advocate's Opinion 35
The Meaning of Life in August 38
A Matter of Taste 41
The Hushberry Season .44
Dancing the Moose 47
Passion Below Zero 50
Ain't She Sweet 52

1991
It Ain't Right, But It's Fine 57
Problems in Communal Living 60
The Season of the Hag .63
Askew 65
No Bird is an Island 67
The Beginning 70

An Echo in the Forest 72
Call of the Wild 75
Colors 78
Tracking Well 81
Just Trees 83
Bad Timing 85

1992

Eclipse 89
The Hollow 92
An Opera of Swans 94
Pig-Wing Blackbirds 97
Settling In 99
Easter Blushes 101
We Have Met the Enemy 104
Renaissance in May 107
Halfway Home 110
Wagons Full of Wishes .114
Epiphany 117
Quicksilver and Gold 119
She Did Not Smile So Well 121
Empty Nest and Conepiles 123
On the Frontier 126
Lunacy 129
Dragons and Tigers and Chickadees 131
Lanterns 134
The First Storm 137
Winter 139
Snowspell 141

1993

A Break 145
New World in One Week 148
A Line to Ourselves 151
Sharing 153

Parole 157
Shangri-La 160
Just Right 163
A Shadow of Summer .167
An Armful of Sunshine 170
Persephone in Full Bloom 173
Once in a Blue Moon .176
Order Out of Chaos 179
Venus's Honey 182
Frost and Fever 185
Shed a Leaf, Shed a Tear 188
The Long Nights Begin 190
Waiting 193
The White Lady 196

1994

The End of the Rainbow 201
Facing the Light 204
The Caretakers 206
Assumption of Risk 209
March Winds 212
Grace 215
Room with a View 218
Good Catch 221
Getting Independent .224
The Moose 227
Transport 230
Others 233
Gold and Harmonies .236
Cutting a Deal 239
Beauty Rides the Beast 241
Knowing How 243

INTRODUCTION

I first met David Hays several years ago while I was on a fishing expedition to the Henrys Fork of the Snake River. I was camped along the edge of the Box Canyon, twenty or so miles west of Yellowstone at the far eastern edge of Idaho— a high, wild country, more than six thousand feet above sea level, often swept by storms encountering the stair-step barrier of the Yellowstone plateau.

While I was fishing the river just below the campsite, my companion, Debra Kronenberg, stayed behind to play her harp. David came striding along the riverside trail; a broad-shouldered, shaggy man with twinkling eyes, dressed in cotton broadcloth shirt and felt hat. We soon discovered that this rough frontier character was none other than the editor, publisher, and Chief Cook and Bottle-washer of the *Island Park Bugle*, off on a foraging expedition for herbs, and always alert to the sound of wood-nymph music.

The *Bugle* is an amazing little newspaper. Our habit was to purchased a copy of this weekly upon reaching Last Chance, Idaho. Originally I bought it for the fishing news, but we soon developed a craving for the entertaining editorials written by Seldom Seen (David); wise, witty, and intensely personal essays of life in a place that most only pass through during the brief but delightful summer. Eventually, as many others have also done, we subscribed by mail, primarily for the delight of David's writings. [*The Bugle*, PO Box 57, Island Park, ID 83429 $20/year postpaid]

An aside here: Last Chance really does exist, although many road maps fail to identify it. It is a named place within the incorporated area known as Island Park, a few miles east of Harriman State

Park (Railroad Ranch). Island Park gives map-makers fits: it is over thirty miles long and two blocks wide, spread along each side of US 20, the major route to Yellowstone from Idaho. Apparently, Island Park was incorporated early in the century, when Idaho's laws authorized certain forms of gambling, but only within incorporated areas. The citizens of the area, with their various tourist-based businesses strung along miles of rural highway, and being of uncommon resourcefulness—then as now, as David's essays attest—decided to incorporate to take advantage of the law. Most maps today show Island Park as a single spot, but then, the map is not the place.

Lesser Frogpond, David's estate, is a single room cabin, heated with wood, insulated with books, and devoid of most 'modern' conveniences—the single concession being electricity for lights and his ten year old computer. No running water—but then, as David has remarked, unless your hobby is plumbing, keeping water liquid at -50° can become a full time endeavor.

The essays collected here were first published between 1989 and 1994 as editorials in the *Bugle*. After many long debates, we have chosen to present them in chronological order. The book is divided into yearly sections, and essays were selected by Debra from the weekly columns of each year. These are presented in the order in which they first appeared.

David shares with his readers the insights of a man who lives in a state of intentional simplicity, and on the terms presented by nature. He tells of life in a severe yet beautiful place; of the largely fearless wild creatures; and—always—of the long, deep, and dominating winter of the high Rockies. He shows by example how great passion of place and spirit can provide sufficient warmth for one to cohabitate with the White Lady. Enjoy.

Dan Casali,

Publisher

1989

A NEW BEGINNING

"All you need to know," he answered, "is I am
building a new privy, and it is not a two-holer."

I suppose I am a peasant. Complicated things that excite others merely confuse me. I am a large, square-bodied, graying man who is stubborn as a stone, though steady enough in purpose and principles. Elegant devices and sophisticated machinery with many shining buttons befuddle me. I can find my way up the mountain in a blizzard, but were you to open the hood of my truck I could not find the fire wall without a map. Perhaps it comes of being born sturdy in the full heaviness of spring, of poor people who were close to the land but never owned any; who were never idle long enough to gather into themselves the complexities and subtle emotional patterns we are so fond of in modern life. I know the mind of a hawk and can read the moods of bears, but I become lost on the trail to another human's heart.

Mine is a very fine life, blessed by the absence of anguish or tragedy and filled with the comfort of knowing my own boundaries. I have a small newspaper that is enormously enjoyable to run and, I am told, fun to read. I write this on a porch I have known for years though it now sits on land new to me and it, a gentle bench looking over a quiet swale groved in young aspen. My companions are an old black cat—with me since I came to these mountains—and a bestiary of other species, compatible in their calmness. This is a secure place. The door is rarely closed and no one is caged, or obligated, or here because they cannot be somewhere else. Some stay, some migrate in their time and season, and some are merely passing through and resting at safe harbor. All are welcome and abide the house rule that none eats the other or becomes wickedly critical of another's ways.

But there is a quiet sadness at evening or by moonlight, for none of us are paired; partnered in that wonderful duality of like kind that so energizes and excites the outside world. We are solitaries, bonded merely by trust and familiarity rather than passion.

Perhaps that is why our life in and around this small cabin is uncomplicated and even often serene. Without the sophisticated complexities of courtship, the daily rhythms fall into dignified habits of "please" and "thank you" between the furred ones and the feathered ones and the slightly balding, quiet owner. Without the gasping gush of hormones and the fierce territorial mating displays, we can all live beside the other in polite, if sexless, companionship. None go hungry or cold, none are required to be brutal or unkind, none have to be sorry for hurtful things done while being driven by despair. It is the peace of passivity, the self-control of the monk who has denied the other Half of a Whole so pregnant with madness.

So I have chosen the simplicity of the peasant, at least for the moment, just as those on my porch and in the tree by the east window have chosen to make the arena of life smaller; to tidy up the problems and duties, to each farm a garden for one, partnerless. We may not know the ecstasies of joining with a mirrored flesh or the deep mingling of shared old age, but we know each other well enough to sense connection and not feel alone. I look out at the land with recognition: fireweed for coming autumn, chokecherry for cough, the coon in the ripe huckleberries, the high kestral seeing through the trees to the distant river, the woodrat turning securely in its bed in the loft, the season told on by the wind, the time by the moon. It is a very fine life.

Yet on a night very recently, I heard one of the wounded companions (it will heal), keening softly in the cabin's single chair. It cried softly, so as not to disturb the others, for the mate now lost and gone. It was very cold that night. I was very cold that night.

GROWING OLD GRACEFULLY

A short while back, in a frenzy of defoliation, I was giving myself the semi-annual (spring and autumn) haircut with the hog shears and noticed that this summer had definitely put the grey to me. I am not normally a person that looks carefully at myself: I have a beard and don't shave, my teeth get brushed without reflection, and my hair (what remains of it) is there for keeping the wind out and the sun off and does not require careful attention before a looking glass. But in an attempt to not be lop-sided and to keep both ears by noting their geography before applying the blades, I was looking in a mirror and was rather startled to see this elderly person peering back at me.

Please note that I am not offended by grey hair—I earned every silver wisp, thank you. I consider dignified my permanent facial lines (gorges) that would do the San Andreas fault proud, and applaud the experts (mostly ladies I have known) who put them there. It is merely that the face was unfamiliar, though not a bad face in its haggard way—I just didn't remember that face being mine.

I pulled out my driver's license to check my advanced age (42), arthritically scratched an area that was once muscle, and wheezed a sigh. How the mighty have fallen! I mused. I curled a lip at the geezer in the mirror and grew thoughtful with what was left of my memory.

I have often heard the phrase about "growing old gracefully" and now, with one foot in the rest home, I realized what a cursed lie that was. I know many folk who are gracefully old but I'll bet my last jar of rheumatism ointment that when they found themselves in my position they weren't very graceful about growing into it. I never considered myself vain (do any of us?) but as I looked on the pathetic remains of a fine, though misspent, youth in the mirror, my vanity was terminally injured. Why, I could have sworn that last week I was still eighteen. How time flies. A noise escaped my throat that sounded suspiciously like a whine.

I pulled what was left of me together and considered the alternatives to my condition. I could think of only one alternative to getting old and that seemed rather final, morbid and unattractive on this fine day (it is snowing hard with the wind out of the north). My cabin doesn't even have running water, so looking for a time machine seemed out of the question. After some thought and bouts of self-pity, I opined that going back was not an alternative, even if possible. I have often heard it said by people (they had probably just been cutting grey hairs for the first time) that they would love to be twenty again if they only knew what they knew now.

Baldergast—my twenties were a horror show of confusion and unguided hormones and I know that because of what I know now, going back wouldn't help that. We are all a collection of histories and failures, large guilts and small exquisite joys, shared hopes and marvelous successes only valued and known in retrospect. The eyesight may be failing but we are getting much more sly about what we see and how we see it. I have paid my dues to get here and am too tired and too grateful to pay those dues again. I wouldn't do it all over differently because I am not sure I understand the Plan and Script, then or now. My hell, I wouldn't even go back to last week, now that I think about it.

It has all been just fine, thanks. I got mostly what I deserved (ouch) and every once in a small while what I wished for. Maybe the best part about getting old is I am much more careful about what I wish for—the Genie was too often the Joker when I was a youth.

I wrinkled a wink at the codger before me, limped back to work, and will stay away from mirrors until spring.

HOME

Sometimes these things happen quite suddenly: I awoke at dawn in my small cabin to find the first big snowstorm had come quietly in the night and given me a home. I looked out at the gentled forest and knew my heart had come to rest in these mountains, completely invested in the seasons and rhythms of this place before all others. Though not mine by birth-right or history I now had roots—this valley had claimed and kept one who had always thought he would be, and die, a pilgrim.

I live at the end of a road. I chose it to be so because I am neither social enough to require companionship nor rude enough to deny it, and if you live at the end of a road folk rarely drop by without serious reason. But the symbolism of living at the end of a road has always nagged me some and frequently made me look over my shoulder down the years.

I was born by the sea but was never of it; it moved too much to kindle my imagination and its protean moods depressed me. The mountains were so far off in my childhood that they were merely a ripple on the eastern horizon, but I spent many summer days watching the clouds build there and dreamed of going.

I went. It has been a very long and twisted road to this place and I have been often lost and afraid. I have been to foreign lands and learned their languages and ways, been to northern Montana at sixteen to harvest wheat on the endless prairie, worked the tow boats in New Orleans, lectured at Columbia University, sang the blues in Memphis. I have cared deeply and often, given my heart away a hundred times never to have it taken…until now.

I live at the end of a road in a place called Last Chance, and since last week the irony has become amusing and I am troubled no more by where to go seeking. I can see the Tetons from my front door and feel the roots of this land lain gently across my days. It is a season to be thankful and I dearly, dearly am.

The pilgrim has come home.

1990

THE DREADED CABIN FEVER

You cannot be alone in spring. Even after the months of isolation, even after you have decided that you are the last intelligent survivor of the Perilous Thaw, even after the Fever has come on you so strong that you have made the path to the cabin a minefield to make sure you are the last survivor, even after all that—the world comes knocking at your attitude and asks if you can come out to play.

I had finally decided that a life of self-pity and personal anguish was perfectly normal and healthy when I stepped out on the porch only to be mugged by a swarm of chickadees. The little beasties chirped and fluttered in every ear to let it be known that they were bored and out of peanut butter. I sloshed some on the outside windowsill next to my bed (chickadees make fine alarm clocks for those that rise at dawn), gracing the birdsong with a few personal snarls, just to make sure they knew I was not about to be put in a good mood. The cat opened an eye and moved two small hairs on the end of his tail.

The cat and the chickadees have an arrangement. He is old and grown winter-fat (people are like their pets, they say), but it is necessary to his self-image and masculinity to kill something now and again—an attitude I am familiar with at this time of the year. The small birds winter with us and every month or so, out of compassion perhaps, they draw straws or something and toss one of the old, or sick, or demented of their flock—while I am not looking—at the old cat, making sure the distance is convenient so that the murder doesn't require too much effort. I have seen pictures of penguins doing the same for killer whales, and caribou for wolves. Idaho politicians do something like this frequently. Since I have no neighbors at this time of year, I am not offered this simple joy. Chickadees are the most cheerful and charming of small birds which is, of course, disgusting to anyone in full Fever, so I waved them off and stepped back through the door into the smoky gloom.

Inside was a fly. No one knows where the flies come from at this time of year. You never see a maggot, it was below zero this week, and you go all winter fly-less. These are not young flies—being about the color, shape and size of an eggplant with wings. These are not even normal flies—they are constructed of rubber and teflon. I have hit one of these spring flies with a full extension, tournament-winning forehand, the swatter gripped perfectly in my fist, and had the fly bank-shot off the wall and come back by my ear sounding like an unguided chainsaw, only to vanish (until you turn out the lights to go to sleep) back into that secret spot where it has been hiding all winter, no doubt chuckling to its fly-self. I have stomped on one of these flies with a new well-pegged set of logging boots (all of me in them) only to see it crawling, menacingly, across the floor at me later in the evening. The Fly from Hell. I have considered a shotgun but it would ruin the insulating quality of my walls, which is poor at best, and still probably not kill the damn thing. This one I netted by hand and tossed into the woodstove, where it will still surely be in August, buzzing a merry tune while roasting marshmallows.

Finally there came a morning too full of not-being-alone to ignore. This morning the year had finally grown old enough, the sun high enough, to wash my bed in sunbeams. I stepped out and listened to the bird music. The flies symphonized gaily in the iron stove. The old cat finally moved all of its cat-pieces at the same time and joined me on the porch. The air was morning-sharp, the coffee had a fine bite, and everything smelled quietly green. The snow melted in the sunshine with small cracklings, and just below that sound I could hear the roots murmuring to each other and stirring in their beds. A non-sacrificial chickadee sunned itself on a ski tip and the cat leaned onto my leg with a breezy purr. I looked up and out, then farther out, and saw the hawk coming home from the south. The Fever passed.

THE POET WHO DIED OF SPRING

Spring is such an assertion of life—the swift mating of birds, the surge of bright flowers, the damp smell of green growing—that it is a puzzle why it should be such a violent and dangerous season for a few among us.

Chatterton, the poet, died in the spring of an eternal mystery called love. There is a fine and powerful painting by Henry Wallis of the Pre-Raphaelite School showing Chatterton laid long on the bed of his tiny London loft, pale of his own death, the bottle of poison empty by his hand, a dark sonnet to the woman who had scorned him gripped in the other hand. The room is filled with spring sunbeams.

Those who found Chatterton were puzzled. The famous and successful man, who was so young as to be nearly a boy, had chosen too fine a day to die. The small loft was cheery with bird-song and swollen with sunlight that had been pushed through the blossoms of the ancient pear tree that stood just outside the un-shuttered window. His world of mid-1800's England was cluttered with women who rivaled for his attention. Why had he chosen so glorious a day to draw such a final curtain over the light?

One morning, in the spring, I sat reading beside a window in my cabin and watched a robin trying to beat itself to death against its reflection in the glass. Nothing I could do would stop the robin from its frenzy of self-destruction. The bird was overwhelmed with spring, driven and compelled by a rhythm in the genes that had gone, ever so slightly, wrong. It could not stop the dance it had begun and was dying of spring.

I finally trapped the bird and released it far away—more for my own comfort than its own. But Chatterton, the poet, had no one to release him and he could not endure the spring. It was not so much the poison that he took that took him, nor even the worm that he called love that chewed at his heart. The season had flung him against himself at a time when something had gone, ever so slightly, wrong. Chatterton died of the overwhelming scent of pear blossoms.

Poets live behind small walls. It is their nature and trade to be exposed and vulnerable. If the walls between them and the world are too sturdy then their words become too thin; you cannot dilute or peer safely at passion without the emotion becoming trivial. If you would be safe and happy then sit quietly by the stove in winter when the trees have choked off the sap to the leaves and your feelings are securely tucked away. But if you would risk feeling passion and joy then you must take your place and sit with the rest of the orchestra during spring and not miss a beat, not sound a false note, while the whole season swells with joined music.

Shelley, the poet, died in spring. He could not swim and was terrified of water, but—for the lack of a special woman—he took a small boat and sailed far out into a lake in Switzerland during a spring gale, and drowned. Dylan Thomas, the poet, built walls of beautiful words around his poor mad wife to protect her, and when, finally, the lyrics failed, he—who was terrified of madness—drank himself insane and died one April in spring. George Gordon, the poet, who was also called Lord Byron, became entangled in one of the many obscene wars between the Greeks and the Turks and charged up a hill against the enemy with a rifle he knew was empty and died on a May morning in the spring rain. Byron was already famous for swimming (impossibly—he had a club foot) the Straits of Bosporus, also in spring, to impress a woman he cherished. He spent the night before the charge around a fire in the company of a man, whose name I have forgotten, who escaped the carnage—minus a leg—and later wrote about Byron talking of a woman and reading aloud the poems he had written to her. She would accept neither his poems nor his passion. At dawn Byron rose from the fire in a marvelous humor, wrote the Journal-Keeper, and said, "But of course it is not the woman, it is the season and it is me," and went up the hill to, like the robin, throw himself fully into the dance.

It has become popular in modern times to see these men, these poets, as too forever young, too adolescent in their compulsive passions, their lives reeking of high drama. But spring is for the young, even the making of young, and passion has become an embarrassing, uncomfortable word only in recent years. It has also become popular in modern times to be compulsive about the gathering of shiny technological toys and the distractions that allow us to make a jest of commitment and cull our feelings down to emotional small change. Of course these poets were fools, or at least foolish—certainly Byron knew it—but it is spring, and its grand orchestra of passionate foolishness, that allows the gift of an only and unique joy not found in other seasons.

We of the mountains also live behind thin walls and are especially capable of hearing spring music. These days I rise before dawn, always. This year, for some reason, I have often sat in the dark and listened to the almost-morning outside. Without opening the door, I can tell what the day will be like, what time of the day it is, what time of the year. The wind brushes one side of the cabin for fair weather, another side for coming storms. One kind of bird, a nighthawk I think, calls in the deep dark until the finches take over at cockcrow. In spring the south wind is more insistent and rising, the birdsong joining the orchestra at first light in a crescendo of mating calls and answers. If I am not very careful, I will begin to feel my pulse search up and down the scale for the harmonies and rhythms and feel a terrible, terrifying need to join the chorus. This is not the aggressive, self-important rut of autumn; it is the compelling, demanding unfolding of spring. The opening of the bud. The unfolding of the self to another. The need to be in step with a dance you cannot do alone.

Spring is the season of peril and promise. Too many false notes and you may die of pear blossoms, but if you find the true melody, there is no other season that can offer such high passion.

TROUT CONNECTION

Even through polarized lenses, the man squints across the flashing riffle as the fish emerges, throwing off jewels of water, and captures the fly. The line tightens, then the reel screams as the trout reaches its body completely out of the water into the late afternoon sunlight and falls, in the agony and love of the possessed, back into the river. It is a passion—perhaps for both—this sudden mating at the ends of an impossibly thin line. The fish has been suddenly wooed, seduced and taken by a feathered pretty, a carefully crafted bauble. But the man had long ago fallen for the fish.

When I first came to these mountains I felt that I might appear silly if I merely stood out in the middle of the river and gaped in awe at the surroundings, so I took a rod with me to try to cover up the rather pole-axed look of a man who had finally found his home. To further the deception I learned how to cast, after a fashion. I used a number ten elk-hair Caddis in a very light pattern so that I could easily see when it was time to cast again while I was oggling the passing eagle or upstream moose. One day, against my best efforts, I caught a fish. I was not surprised—I was astonished. Some kind of fine and wonderful magic ran from the fish, up the line, through my hand and into my heart. It locked the mountains to me and made me kin to a community of rivers and forest that I have never left. A moment of fish had brought my spirit home.

Perhaps it is so with those who hunt deer in the autumn-red willows, or the young lovers besotten with spring under our freeing sky, or the older pair in Last Chance who sit holding hands on their porch near the evening river. I hope so. It is a special feeling, but not unique. I have seen it in the eyes and carriage of other men and women who live and visit here. These mountains are a special place and call out the special in each of us.

Fly fishing is a unique way to make love with the mountains. It transcends the predator-prey relationship and brings dignity to both the man and the fish. It is not a team sport (though you might argue the point this weekend) and brings a person to that place within which lies above competition or scores. You cannot present a fly well with aggression or bully a fine fly rod with success. You step into the river and leave much behind—many things too serious, many problems too worn. There is no more real world than the sunlight and the riffle and the waiting fish. There is no more important thing than the moment and the ballet of cast and drifting fly. This is to be enjoyed. This is to be done with found grace. This is the real world.

Since I have made a career of being poor, I have only two fly rods, both given to me by friends. One is a spring-grass green Winston, a nine-and-a-half for a five, that is more art than merely a device. I often lack the delicacy to handle it well, but on wind-quiet evenings when the fish need to be whispered to, I have sometimes lifted out everything I ever hoped I could be through and beyond that rod; the line arcing like a wish to a pool swollen with trout. But often the Winston asks too much of me and I am not proud enough to fish it often or well.

The other rod is a seven-and-a-half for whatever. It is a rough fireplug of a rod that Mike Lawson built for himself—he was twelve or thirteen, I think he said—with a mail order Shakespeare blank, and it has seen much rough travel in canoes and truck beds. I admired it in his shop one day and he dignified my greed by making me a present of the old rod.

I am very happy with this rod. Like me, it is not aristocratic enough for fancy moods and is serviceable and enduring without being pretty. But it does not lack the magic. Once during the early joys of the green drake hatch the rod and I were prowling the off-bank channels near Pinehaven. The fish were in that emotional state that bull elk suffer during the fall rut—all want and little caution. I false-casted several times searching for that one true presentation that could not be ignored or denied. Suddenly a fish broke the surface and time shocked into slow-motion. The paradrake fly was fully two-and-a-half feet above the water, pinned to the end of the line. The fish rose in inches away from the water like a loved hope. The fish began to fly, fly damnit, toward the paradrake. It grabbed the piece of fluff and still kept going. The line snapped taut, the rod and my wrist held, and I opened my mouth to let the heart bark out a Great Shout.

There are special moments when everything is just right. After a very long, beautiful time, the fish came back to the water and challenged the relationship. No one hesitated or thought things over or planned the contest; from fish to line to rod to heart, all the elements of the dance came together. The fish flew twice more and the rod and I bowed and swayed and rose along. It was not a large fish—sixteen or seventeen inches perhaps—but it was a brave fish, a Hemingway fish, a fish of large heart. I realized, through my consuming joy, that if we danced much longer the lactic acid build-up would kill the fish so I stopped the magic and horsed it in on the short bulky rod. After carefully removing the hook I looked at the fish I so admired, kissed it fully on the lips, and placed it back in the water. True love is letting go. True story.

TOM

His name was Tom Bailey and he was my grandfather. There can be no more American name than Tom Bailey and I still carry his first name in the middle of mine, David Thomas Hays. Many years ago his heart skipped just a little and he went to a doctor who looked at him and saw only a large weathered old man and did not look carefully enough. He gave Tom a drug to keep his heart from skipping, but the drug and the doctor were wrong, and his heart stopped forever instead. His wife and remaining children will read this, as I will, and remember some moments of the man that came across the years and summoned me to tears this morning in the mountains.

There were once the summers of my Golden Age when my father would have to go build and fly the nation's aircraft in a place we could not go, so my mother would tuck my sister and I in an old car—they were all old cars then—and fetch us back to her family on the God-damned, hard-baked red hopeless soil of western Oklahoma, to the cotton fields and tilting stone houses owned—always—by another man, away from the emotional wasteland of southern California; back miles off the paved roads, jumping the ancient ruts; back to the that-year's farm where Tom and Lottie and their tall skinny proud boys, my uncles, lived by a poor creek flowing through a poor land, and fought the dust—again—that year for a crop they did not own. Even the chickens were thin and tough, pecking at a yard more damned hard and lifeless than the shiny highways I had left so far behind.

It was a rooster of those years that pulled me so near Tom this morning in the Rockies. I rose before dawn and encouraged the fire back out of the ashes and placed the coffee cooking and turned on the radio to see if there were anything I should know or care about this day. A silly commercial came on about something I do not remember, but in the background a rooster crowed, a sound I have not heard in years and suddenly I was so very small and happy, holding tightly to the end of Tom's shirtsleeve—I could rarely hold his hand because there was always a tool there: a hoe, a wrench, an old rifle—as we walked out into the cottonfields, already hellish-hot in the early light of an Oklahoma July day.

For God's Sake, Tom. Why do you have to come calling on a lonely spring dawn in the mountains when I am nearly as old now as you were then? I was no higher than your belt that morning, but now I am just as large and square and unbent and weathered as you. I loved you as only an eldest male grandchild can love a man, but that was a thousand mornings ago and I am now so different, yet so much alike you, as only distance and blood can create. Why that morning to this? It is because there are no mirrors in my cabin here high up by the river this morning, and so moments like this must come to tell me what I cannot see or will not face.

Tom Bailey, the American, the mostly Cherokee but plenty of Scotch-Irish-Cajun-German, stood in the middle of his rented cotton field, even his long dawn shadow not as big as the man he was to me, and gave me the hoe from his other hand, a hoe taller than I was. He reached down and pulled one of his plants aside and pointed, never losing the tool in his hand, never putting it down, ever. There was a small weed under the cotton leaf, near the stem. He moved his face near mine and said that if the weed were this big—moving his hands—we, the boys and the women and he and me, would hoe this morning. If not—moving his hands again—there were other things to do.

We walked down the rows. He moved another leaf and showed me a bug. If there were this many bugs he said—moving his fingers—we would go back to the barn and coax the old Ford tractor to life and thrump-thrump back out to the fields, me in his lap between his chest and the wheel, and spray the crop. If not, there were other things. Perhaps we would take some rotten, smelly things and wrap them in paper and go down to the creek and tease sleepy catfish from the muddy slow water, or move hay in the high cool barn, or climb on the one old horse he was so proud of and ride like kings over the land.

We walked around the farm pond that morning and Tom warned me of the cottonmouth snakes and snapping turtles that small boys are so enchanted by. And finally in the apricot orchard, listening to the slow drone of hornets as they harvested the sweet fallen fruit, I asked Tom if these things were bad, these weeds and snakes and bugs. Were they bad things that we must kill? Tom did not laugh at the belt-high boy that morning, he was more man than that. He did not preach to me because he was not an openly religious man—he did not need to be. But he did not answer right away either. He grew quiet and so did I. It was a serious question, even if asked by a small boy not as high as his belt, and Tom was not a man to give quick answers to serious questions.

That evening in the twilight he finally put his tools down, put them away in their place, and picked me up lightly and set me on the edge of the old stone well. A fairy-tale well to me, so dark and cool and silent when the heavy wooden cover was moved aside. He brought up water for us and began to speak, holding the heavy steel dipper for me:

I would be a man soon enough, he said, and I needed to know these things about good and bad. There are good and bad things in the world, he said, but they are not these things, these weeds and snakes. To get up in the morning and see these things of the coming day's work as good or bad would be troubling and not useful. The work for the day is rarely a thing of good or bad; if there are too many bugs for the crop to do well, they must be killed. If not, a man turns away and does other things. If the snake comes too close, you must either kill it or move yourself away. If not, you must let the snake be and do other things.

There are always other things to be done, not because they are more important or less important, but because it is time to do those things. To think of too many things as good or bad, to try to be judge over all the things of the day, will prevent a man's sleep that night and trouble him until he can no longer see what must be done. The morning, said Tom, will show you what is to be done that day. Do the work that you are called to that day, and rest when evening comes. Life is to be enjoyed, not measured, Tom said.

He pushed the heavy cover back and hung the dipper-tool in its place. Come inside, Tom said, your grandmother will have laid a fine table for supper and your uncles will take their guitars down from the wall when it is time to light the lamps. This day's work is done.

I sipped coffee on my porch and peeked at a corner of the morning Tetons, the cat, who is not belt-high, beside me.

Thank you, Tom. I have been trying to worry myself old when, like you were then, I am already old and perhaps, maybe, thanks to you, wise enough not to worry.

I took the old shovel-tool down from its place and began to pull the winter away from my windows.

SPLENDOR IN THE GRASS

I sat on the porch the other evening early sharing, myself with the mosquitoes and watching the full moon swell up and pull free from the eastern plateau. The moon's path was so low I half expected the rising light to strike sparks from the tips of the Tetons in passing, but it made it and headed south as always. As beautifully, wonderfully always. Spring is in the mountains again, and even the bugs are pretty and welcome. Nothing ever seems to truly end in the mountains, unlike down in the cities where fads and trends and names and lives are changed on a whim—endings coming too soon for some, too late for others.

Even the joy, the glee, of spring has become familiar and looked-for. Through spending the steady time, season to season, and investing the heart always, I have come to look forward and back with equal pleasure. It is spring and that is good and as things should be. Months ago the wind rattled at the north window and snow crept in around the edges of the door and that was fine and proper to the time. Life slowed and slept and woke again this May. In the mountains nothing is ever finished, ever ends.

Last year I left my home of many years near Swan Lake and moved a few miles north to a small piece of land that I own. I left in a flurry of decision—some things are best done quickly—and the very last thing I took from all those years, with the truck running in the driveway, was a small apple tree I had planted near the door in hopes of shared old age. It was a small shoot when I bought it and, like our lodgepole who are so painfully slow until they can stand above the average snowpack, it had not grown much and was still barely three feet tall and thin. The tree had not escaped my year of various horrors and had been broken a few inches above the ground by a stray power tool, an escaping vehicle, a thoughtless-ness, something.

I took the tree to my new land and carefully dug a hole and planted it at the base of a small south-facing cliff of lava rock. Buried it really; I was so sure that it was dead that I muttered the rites of passing as snow kernels chewed at my face on that raw pre-Thanksgiving day. It has ended, I thought, for the small tree clung dryly to its trunk by only a thin strip of bark, and it felt too light in my hand to carry life. Then came a winter too cold, too often, in too many ways.

Last Friday I went down into the swale to pick the young May mint and found the little apple tree stretched along the ground in the wild roses. The tree was full of reaching apple-purple leaves with one small stubborn blossom stationed about midway up the stem. My knees went out and I sat down fully in the roses and tall grass and watered the tree with things that had been carried too long.

There are moments of release in life that are so healing, so cleansing, that they forever change you. I am not being silly—this was not Saul on the road to Damascus—it was merely a broken tree and an aging hermit sharing a few hours and years in the sweet grass of a spring afternoon, but it was as real and brave and true as I will ever enjoy. The moment was not the finish line, of course, or the brass ring, or the bell. Things do not end in the mountains that way, if ever. It was just a confirmation, a hand reaching out of the Somewhere and gripping shoulder and leaf to say: you are doing fine and on the right road. Keep it up.

I saw her the other day, and we talked quietly while the light over her shoulder moved across the aspen outside and up the edges of the mountains behind her. She knows I love her because I have told her so and she both believes me and understands what I have said. We are both wrapped in the mountains and know things that others cannot know. But she chooses not to acknowledge or accept that love, and that is perhaps fine and proper and as it should be. It will not end here or go away; there are seasons to everything.

I looked around her and beyond to the mountains and smiled. This place, my home, is a place where broken apple trees bloom.

PULLING THE PLUG

Some would say that living inside a volcano is risky business. Maybe so, especially since this one is 60,000 years or so overdue for its wake-up call. Ah, you say, but Island Park is not Yellowstone. Of course not. Yellowstone is the frisky dance-hall girl next door who is considerably younger and more prone to letting off pent-up steam than our local Island Park sweetie.

The Island Park caldera, or crater, is perhaps the largest in North America, about 23 by 32 miles—the short side being caused when the more recent Yellowstone eruption flowed over our eastern flank. If you are near The Bugle office or down by Osborne Bridge, you are on several miles of rhyolite and basalt above the core—a plug, really. Remember the Jules Verne story about the men in the stubby bullet who are shot out of the big cannon to the moon? We are much like that.

Now, being 60,000 years overdue in geologic time is like being a few seconds late to the cocktail party, no one is very upset, yet. Major eruptions are signaled by some warning signs like frequent minor earthquakes (there are four to six daily in the Yellowstone—Hebgen—Henrys Lake area) or odd behavior in the soon-to-be-erupted inhabitants (watch a person near you recently, any person), but the event can still only be predicted for sometime between the next fifteen minutes and fifteen hundred years—nothing to lose sleep over. Thrill-seekers should stick to driving the local highway between June and November, and those adept at ignoring things will feel right at home.

I have always liked the idea of the Island Park volcano: it doesn't have the carnival atmosphere of the loud next-door neighbor and is more faithful and serene as a partner. The heart is very deep here and the pulse of the volcano is subtle and various.

There is a vent (or fumerole, or chimney) near the highway on Federal Hill that has an erratic groan to it during its rare appearances. The trappers thought the one out by Lyle Springs smelled of gold. I once heard the several at Ripley Butte sing as sweetly as the Sirens of Odyseus. But my treasure and sanctuary is where I go to lay me down and listen to the world sigh.

There is a gorge up the north fork of Split Creek that is so deep the sunlight only touches bottom for a few hours a day even in the height of summer. A small cold creek rattles down from the edge of the caldera above and the walls of the gorge are stained with the litter of large-taloned hungry birds who nest in the caverns. The North Fork Fire of 1988 tore off the surface forest above the narrow valley, but even the winds get lost in this twisting place and so the creek and the bottom were spared and are still a jeweled riot of greening aspen and blood-red obsidian and exotic wildflowers fed by seeps in the canyon walls. Those walls are stratified rock album pages of a history so much larger than mine that I can feel insignificant and safe beneath them.

Behind a boulder the size of my cabin there is a place of vines and emerald-leafed shadows where sand remains from an ancient stream path that marked a bed before the canyon bent and turned the water away. I make my bed there where there is a crack in the wall and I can hear the earth breath. It is a place to go when I am feeling too large of myself or too harmed for company. The sighs from that deep vein in the planet have moods: passion or despair or melancholy or even indifference. There was once an Oracle at Delphi that sighed messages through just such a crack in the world, for Delphi is also a place of volcanos.

As I dozed the walls rumbled with sighs and I remembered something forgotten. Have you ever been in an earthquake? I have been in several, here and abroad, and they can be terrifying and destructive but there is also a lift of being when the earth moves that is like only one other thing I have felt:

When I was very small, perhaps two or three, my father put me in his lap and pulled the cockpit shut and we started across the salt flats, me looking out the windows at glider wings so long that they seemed to stretch out to the edge of the desert. Then very lightly, like a summer sunrise, there was a lift, a lift of me, the long wings reaching up and turning my small heart to sky. This was not the push and pull and then release of the playground swing or the reluctant acceleration of a fast car. This was lift without friction or pressure, like the perfect note in a song that rises without effort, without tether, the kite beyond the string.

I lay in the dappled afternoon and listened to the crevice sigh and felt the earth move and lift me that way. I sat up and grinned back at a badger peering around the boulder. The canyon wall whispered things. I remembered that I live in a volcano and that I choose to live here. I remembered that this special place and a special person have gifted me with very long wings to lift myself. So I came out of the dark valley of Split Creek and went home.

A CREVICE IN TIME

Summer. The full bloom of the year. From my porch I watch a pale wild rose elbowing in the wind at a sage bush while a dragonfly perches nearby waiting to hover bluely in the between space. The squirrel and the finches gobble at the seed dish like wild vikings trying to outfeast each other, flinging husks and excess under the table to the napping chipmunks. The midsummer, midday sun charms the foxtail grass a few more inches out of the ground. It is a busy day in the mountains in a busy, living world.

It is on bright July days, while I rest puddled in the heat with the cat on the porch, that I wonder why we humans, as a species, seem to hold life so lightly, so carelessly; why we make of life a trinket of shallow value.

Oh, I am not thinking of hunters and animal rights and endless war: some of my favorite companions make a living of eating each other and sparring over territory in season. The finch makes a meal by filching the infant seed from the bosom of the cone, and even the meadow weed nurses at the soil. No, I am thinking of your life, and too often my life, and how we waste time on the trivial and petty moments, moments that soon accumulate into a cache of regret. Time is a thing, the angel-haired man from Princeton said, and like all things it will pass: that moment forever, this moment soon, the coming moment never.

I, of course, on this hot July day, on the porch, watching the tip of the cat's tail search for a stray breeze, cannot be accused of idle loafing. I make a living having idle thoughts on hot July days. It is important to my profession to swelter over my species from my porch. I am fully committed to porching this afternoon and not causing disappointment to my audience of flies. I am working hard.

Still, it is curious that you (yes, and me) invest so much time in angered concern over each other, as if we had nothing better to do. A moment ago the porch squirrel complained loudly as another vagrant squirrel dared eye the Ritz, but I doubt if tonight the squirrel will complain loudly, and at length, in hindsight about the incident as a larger squirrel on a barstool did recently to me. I have had the honor, these last years, of having been bitten by an astonishing number of large, furred species, but I doubt if they dwell on my injury in their winter groves and caverns or plot further maiming of me. I cannot picture a club of January moose sitting around the stove chewing cud over old insults and slights and wrongs.

From the throne of my porch I see things this way: For some distance down through the swale and beyond, this summer afternoon shimmers in varied and eager green. In the best of years the growing season in Island Park is only 100-120 days long. The green and growing things in my yard are sprinter weeds, olympic wildflowers, serious grasses, intent berrybush, solid hard-working Republican pines. They are at their business at dawn and frisky for their time here. The days are important to them, the life the days make is valuable to them. From seed swollen with purpose to spring sprout and hot July bloom and autumn's seed again, it is a festival, it is a party, it is a celebration—but there is little time for bickering and the flowering will not wait for a few choice moments of character assassination.

Last week while touring my landed holdings, I pressed some creeping dogbane (what a fine name!) aside and found a tree growing from the rock cliff. I looked closely and found a crevice so thin that I could not push even my smallest finger within it. From the crack was growing a common bedraggled-looking lodgepole pine about three inches in diameter and seven feet long, with erratic clumps of green needles here and there along its span. The tree was possessed of some years because the bark was gray and scaled like the feet of old birds and the trunk was knobby and bent.

I admit that I gaped at the tree and was eye-wide astonished at its will to live and grow. Here am I: a complainer by trade, a whiner over love lost or never obtained, a literary companion to sorrow over lacking a companion, facing a tree about my own age which was growing greedily from a my-belt-high crack in stone that probably contained less soil than the rug in my cabin. It was embarrassing. I was shamed by the gnarled tree's grip on what it had been offered: a chance for life in a crack and the seed-wise sense to use the time to grow—sip the snowmelt passing through the crevice, reach for the sunlight this July day, store strength and sleep long in the winter. No whining; just do much with the little given.

The Gift is in the Giving

The fellow stopped yakking long enough to suck in some air (a shame, since it no doubt prolonged life) and fumble around in his shirt pocket. He had been holding forth for too long on the secrets of fly fishing and other woodwise-ish stuff, though I'll bet if the conversation had turned to astro-navigation or muffin baking he would have still been right in there. He made much use of the surrounding air to herd his point and pushed beer cans around the bar as props to the drama. I wondered if the barstool had a seat belt or whether he had just been there long enough to take root.

"I tell you" (he did) "You've never see anything like this special fly. That hog in the Box Canyon was on it before I even had it tied on the leader." He produced something from his pocket and held it out for inspection.

It really was amazing. I had never seen a piece of carpet lint on a hook before. Or maybe it was a piece of insulation the squirrel had pulled loose from the roof. On a hook.

"Never seen anything like it," I said with heavy neutrality.

"Course not, Rube!" he quacked. "My special invention it is, just for this river and these conditions. Here, you have this one, I can always tie more."

Rube? Given these conditions I considered patting him thankfully on the wrist while I placed the invention in his exposed artery. Rube? I have spent years carefully cultivating this manly and rugged image and now, by Gerty, this semi-bacterial upright road-kill decided I had just stepped off the bus.

I purchased a beer, placed it in the face of the oaf for silence, and started in on the one about me and the grizzly bear and the dull can opener and my tentmate's curling iron. The audience was just warming up as I got to the part about the trout stampede and the moose when the fire went out of me, I got disgusted, and had to cut it short with a brief description of fencing off the wolverines with my Winston rod and her running off with the fresh-curled orangoutang. I bought a round for the heathens and slipped out the door.

We spend a lot of time selling ourselves to each other. It's unseemly behaviour and, at best, never seems to buy anyone anything. The boor at the bar was afraid to stop the sales pitch, even though he probably knew he was offensive and boring, because even derisive attention is better than no attention at all. Then I got my feelings ruffled and decided to let loose with a full blown version of the Brag: that grand Rocky Mountain tradition of my yarn being bigger than your yarn. I was selling something too, and I have seen and done that under a lot of other circumstances.

I suppose there are just too many reasons—none of them good—for putting yourself on the market: insecurity, intolerable onlyness, marking territory with bluff; a hundred cravings that make us socially vulnerable enough to appear on the menu. Watching the auction too often finally put some meaning to a word used often in and about our mountains:

Solitude. It is a cliché attached to the high forest that you can find peace and quiet joy in the 'solitude' here. Perhaps it is because, unless you are very more complicated than most, you cannot sell yourself to a tree or chipmunk. Removed from the pressure of pretense, we can settle back into something more emotionally comfortable. What is curious is that it takes a myth—that being alone, in solitude, is a fine acceptable thing in the mountains—for people to take a break from the market mentality. It would seem more simple to just go to a quiet room and close the door and be alone for some thoughtful hours. That so many people cannot do that, without the excuse of the mountains, might mean that they have not sold themselves well enough to themselves to tolerate their own unchaperoned company. So we seek ourself in others, live in a world of needed mirrors, and trust our own worth to the judgement of strangers.

Even wilderness solitude does not always offer peace. Around the 5th century some very pious early Christians tired of the bustle of metropolitan North Africa and retired, each alone, to some caves in the huge treeless mountain ranges near Tripoli, to become the legendary Desert Fathers hermits. One of them kept a lengthy and beautiful journal where, in the early years of his cavehood, I read of him trying to sell himself to God. He was not worthy, he was too worthy, he was just right—if only he could get the sales pitch right, God would have him. Finally, nearly ten years into his exile, he gives in, gives up, and gives himself away: no price, no haggling, he made himself a gift to his God. From then on the journals become melodic and whimsical and serene; the Desert Father had found himself when he stopped looking, had been received when he stopped asking.

The concept is so simple—too simple certainly for me to remember and live by: from nearly anywhere in Island Park it is a short distance to the trees where you can sit in the late July sunlight alone for awhile, watch the fireweed shake off the dust in an afternoon breeze, and give yourself to the wealth of the moment. After you have done that, you may find it is an even shorter distance to someone you love, where you can do the same thing and be received. The mountains will help you remember.

AN ADVOCATE'S OPINION

I guess I need a back door in the office; you know, an escape hatch to bail out of when I see trouble coming that I'm going to get into. But I don't have a back door, and the windows are still winter-sealed (we're a little slow on the chores sometimes), so…

A Big City Salt Lake television crew showed up in town the other day and nosed up and down the road looking for someone to go on camera and say ten or sixteen things about the big hydroelectric project that has been proposed for the Island Park Dam. They of course have a right to ask such penetrating, news-worthy questions, but the TV folk seemed a little surprised that many townspeople considered it equally their right not to answer those questions, at least on the record. Finally some local wag pointed them at my door and they arrived trailing cables and microphones and deadlines. They were nice enough people—a little harried and fluttered—but they were all right. They had a nice polite dog, so they were all right.

They asked if I had any opinions about the dam project. I said sure, opinions are my trade and baggage, no problem. Was there a problem going on the record about it? No problem, I said, I'm a on-the-record sort of guy, even when I talk in my sleep. How 'bout going on camera? I didn't like that much. I wear a beard so I don't have to shave and therefore look at myself too often. I'm shy about pictures because when I see them I don't know who the funny guy is. Even when I do know, I don't know who the guy is. But anything to help the homefront so sure, just spell Island Park right and don't get personal. I fluffed what's left of my hair and powdered my nose for the lights.

How about the politics, they asked? I don't know about the politics. I know where the bill is and I know who the dignitaries are who are being as noisy as a pack of Sandhills over the thing, but I limit my politics to dogfights with County Commissioner Siddoway and other friends. I don't like to get rude farther than I can throw a large phrase.

Do we need the hydroelectric project, they asked? No, I don't need it personally, I said. They didn't like that.

Does Island Park need the project, they asked? No, I said, Fall River Electric is real good about getting us power most of the time and the electricity generated would be sold out-of-state I'd read. The economic impact of the construction wouldn't be much of a deal except maybe Saturday nights, I said.

How did I feel about the whole thing? I thought we ought to shoot all the people and feed fertility drugs to the bears, I said. Get serious, they said. Look, I said, I warned you when you came in the door: It's the full moon, it's hotter than a green-eyed Cajun girl and has been for days, it's how I feel, and if one of you will hold the camera, we can use the other for bait and see how things are.

Hey, I said, I'm hot and tired and so are you. Point your camera, stop asking questions, and I'll give you sound bites and answers. I don't like the dam thing. They That Hold The Wires think they might need the power capacity here in the northwest sometime in the next ten or twenty years. Let's get local: we of Island Park are worried about getting to next week and are not big on If and Maybe. The dam thing has got good friends spouting political ideology at each other that went out twenty years ago. Hell, even eastern Europe gave up that kind of nonsense last year.

It's like this, I said: If they don't build the thing, it is not going to be a matter of huge consequence. If they build it the way they say, maybe it might be all right and maybe somebody in southern California will know and remember to say Thank You, Island Park when they turn on the light switch. But if they goof even an itsy little bit we might as well re-name the Henrys Fork the Humpty Dumpty because sorry isn't going to be good enough. It will annihilate the local economy. Since you already took all our wood and shipped it to Japan and since you sent your market hunters up to kill our elk and poach our lakes, why don't you go up on Black Canyon where our trees used to be and set out solar cells on the clear cuts and steal all the electricity you want out of our sky?

I love this river and it is part of my home. If it ain't broke, don't fix it. You think maybe you might need the electricity sometime. I think for certain I want this river full of fish and friends—and I'm not alone. You may think I'm just another furry madman who has been up too high too long, but I know a fellow who fights it out on the floor of the Stock Exchange in New York every day and comes to this river two weeks out of the year to get sane—and he is not alone, there are thousands of him. They live here in their dreams and they come here out of love and need and maybe, just maybe, they need a healthy river bright with fish even more than I do.

I get a case of the careful squints when I hear someone speak of Island Park as a resource. It is indeed; I have spent a lot of years as an advocate of the Island Park area, and that resource is hospitality. Come take what you need: meat, pleasure, peace, sanity, whatever. But don't take what you don't need. And don't be so arrogant as to think you can't make a mistake up in this wild country, I've made plenty. God has a funny sense of humor about people who think like that…I know. If you were to flub with your dam thing, it would cost a lot more than money. It would cost an important piece of joy for many that cannot afford to lose that in their lives.

Most of you readers don't get Salt Lake TV up here so I thought you ought to know what I said, even if they don't air it.

I said so… on the record.

The Meaning of Life in August

Mountains and recluses go together, I suppose. It was so in the stories I read as a child; the picture of a fellow who hasn't had a haircut since Saturday ten years ago, perched on his high crag pondering Everything—when he wasn't busy pursuing Princesses and Unicorns. Also part of the same legend is the idea that given enough of their own solitary company and the lack of oxygen on such crags, these fellows became simple in the very old sense of that word (simpleton, simple-minded, and so on). I think I am beginning to understand that part of the myth.

The cat and skunks and I were kicking around this idea back at our home, Hermit's Hovel, last week and came to the firm (and inflating) conclusion that we were right, and much of the behaviour we saw around us was wrong, or at least misguided. Things really are simple; elegantly, beautifully, simple. Any attempt to complicate your life, at least in the mountains (the only context we've had in the last ten years or so), is just a need to delegate responsibility to anywhere but yourself.

We decided (remember it was very hot last week) that it works like this: If you say your prayers at night, put down the lid on the toilet, and eat all the vegetables on your plate, God will find you amusing (or at least unusual) and give you what you want. Oh, not the new truck or cabin or tasteless and futile relationship you've been mulling over. Not that kind of want. But if you keep things simple and restrain the rules you live by to a list small enough not to forget anything, you will be gifted with the thing you wanted so badly that you were afraid to ask for it, even when alone: A life that can be understood, that can be conducted with some small dignity, a life that has more peace than peril, a life that often is visited by sit-down, tingle-ish moments of deep joy.

Things that are complicated can also be confusing and poorly understood. But, thankfully, there are many pieces of living that do not need to be understood. Consider the aspen leaf: very soon perhaps the leaf will begin to turn colors. I cannot any longer remember the chemical formula for photosynthesis, but fortunately the leaf can, and so that intricate transformation will be accomplished without confusing me. I can, however, understand and appreciate the motive: I would not go greenly into an Island Park winter—that would be a foolish struggle I almost attempted once— I would go gold to pleasure the season and the surroundings, then drop off and bud up until spring. Very simple. I do not need to understand the process as long as I can understand and accept the reason.

This is not an excuse or plea for a life of ignorance; ignorance is not bliss, it is a painful, dulling blindness. You do not have to live in a remote area like this to have experienced people who have the arrogance of self-imposed stupidity. It is a reverse elitism to assume, with a huff, that what you do not know is unnecessary trash, and that those who know things you do not are worthless snobs. That kind of contempt is moral suicide, for you will soon strangle your life on your own prideful, chosen boundries.

The simpleton role that we of the summer porch decided was valuable is a thing of control and options. What you are in charge of and what, though you may admire it, you are not in control of. Filling choices and fruitless struggles. I am (sometimes) good at getting the wood in to warm the hovel. The cat is marvelous at controlling the chipmunks when they group up to conduct a viking raid on the pantry. The skunks are in charge of scraps and keeping me alert about where I put my feet at night. The simple life in the mountains is a life of chopping wood and carrying water and minding your own business and keeping promises—especially those made to yourself—and not trying to do or be something you are not equipped for.

I would make a very poor tree, or bear, or skunk. When I pay close attention, I am an adequate human being because that is the equipment that I was given and that is the shape of the magic that flows through me. I discovered very plainly (simply) one frozen February that who I am is very unimportant compared to understanding what these mountains are and how to conduct my life in them.

I cannot presume to teach the leaf how or when to change colors because I have forgotten, if I ever was, how to be a leaf. Once I accept the same principle about the other things about me—like my neighbors and their lives—I will have captured a simplicity that will allow me great joy in simply sitting on my porch in these mountains and chatting with the skunks.

A Matter Of Taste

I discovered recently that I do not have meals—I have daily eating disorders. Perhaps once I was more picky, but now food is not chosen for its texture, taste and succulence; about dusk I glance at the table to see if there is enough square-footage of edible substance to sustain life for the next few hours, and then fall on it like a wolf. Table-prey is preferred that leaves one hand free for turning pages or manipulating typewriter keys. No doubt it is disgusting—even the cat leaves—but I am in the game for the nourishment and not the presentation of etiquette, since I noticed at an early age that the furnace will not cook without fuel.

It is like that when you live alone; meaning, in my case, with no other human about to upturn a nose. It is not ignorance—I know and can use properly all twelve forks to the left of the plate if the company calls for it—it is habit. If I did not make a habit of eating, I probably would not notice the lack until overtaken by the blind staggers and withers.

Once when I was in a noticing mood I figured the huge majority of my time was spent doing things out of habit: fetching the wood, carrying water to the cabin, putting the skunk out and the cat in, things like that. You might think that we of the mountains, with our free and wild life-style and all, would be more free of habitual behaviour than the city cousins who are locked to the clock. Phui. We are worse. Joe Meek—of last century mountain man fame— once tossed a man in the fire because the camp-tender had placed his rifle on the wrong side of his blanket-roll. The mountain life might be wild, but we like our life to have some familiar structure.

And so it is. We cannot stay awake too long without sleep. We cannot stay fully awake when awake for too long without folding under the strain of paying too much attention. So we spend an astonishing amount of time on automatic pilot while the rest of us slips off for a nap. Is that bad? I suppose it depends on who and where you are: A man whose attention is turned off while hiking the south face of Sawtelle Mountain can die from hungry boulders, loose bears, or a foot in the wrong airspace. Good habits can keep you alive: Joe Meek, for instance, wanted his gun by his right hand if the Indians dropped in for tea. Having the woodpile in the same place as last year helps things during a January white-out. Even religious ritual, which is mostly fancified habit, was created so that if God wished to ring you up for a chat, you would be in the right place and mood for the company.

The problem comes when, like almost everything else in life, the habits are carried to excess. While getting through the day you are presented with a number of challenges, to use a nice word. If you are just going through the motions you will, at the very least, miss a lot.

Riddle it this way: You go out and get an armful of wood and bring it in to the stove. You do it a million times. One of those times you picked up a special stick—a real Van Gogh-Picasso piece of wood, so pretty it would make your teeth hurt from grinning too much—but you miss it because you're fetching wood out of habit. Not This piece of wood or That piece of wood, just wood. It's probably not a big deal—much beauty goes un-noticed—since it's just wood, but the same principle applies to the people we wrap our lives in.

Suppose you are fetching idle conversation with someone in the pub or on the porch. This someone has one of those non-physical heart attacks that we are all prey to; an blind-siding anguish or sorrow that makes the eye-edges go just a little taut. Maybe if you reached over and got ahold of a piece of them they could catch their breath and not be crippled for that moment. Nothing dramatic, just a touch to tell them you noticed and therefore cared. The habits that control most of our relations with each other would let something like that go by un-noticed. Too bad.

We try to control the crises and surprises and impossibilities of living by stuffing them into some familiar pattern, something we can recognize. That part is all right until carried to excess and we start doing the same thing to our own feelings and behaviour: habit is not reality, it is not now; habit is what you used to do that worked mostly all right so you kept doing it.

For instance, love is a crisis. Always. It starts out fine: You pluck your heart out, plunk it into someone else's arms and ask them to hang on to it for a while, or forever, or whatever they think best. Very unfamilar stuff, full of surprises and joys and wonderful clumsiness. But it is a lot of hard work to feel that way and since love is almost always resonant, you are holding their heart also. So one day you lose your nerve and snatch the little hummer back and say: Oops! What I meant to say was: you have dinner ready at five and I'll bring home the bacon and we'll share some solid habits we can count on instead of all this frisky freedom nonsense.

So it is. You are back to dealing with wood, instead of This wood or That wood and another beauty slips by un-noticed. Life in the mountains is very demanding and if you do not pay attention well, the bears will eat you. Love is just as demanding, and habits are just as dangerous. The food I ate last night may have been very good food, maybe fine cuisine. I don't know because I didn't taste it while I was eating. Too bad.

The Hushberry Season

It has certainly been true in my time and some of the Village Elders tell me it has always been so: In the heat-height of summer, when we are for a few days above the calming frost, a scruffy bush on our northern shadowed slopes bears a small pill of nectar that is so dearly sweet, so rare of color and taste, that the lower valleys empty their hamlets of pilgrims, the bears emerge from the deep forest, and the birds begin to flock up for the search. Even the mice are in on the hunt. If you see a deeply purple stain on fingertips or beak or muzzle, you know it is the time. But if you ask where the cherished berries are, a deep hush falls over folks and flocks. It is the Hushberry Season.

Vaccinium is the genus name for a group of plants that include the Blueberry, Grouseberry, and our very own Huckleberry. The scrufulous bushes are cousin to the manzanita, what we call here Uva Ursi or Kinni-Kinnick. It is a very unassuming bush, a very quiet rodent of a bush for most of the year, but about now it begins to dangle a treasure that will bring grizzlies twenty miles a day to the berry patches and people from such far distant lands as Argentina and Rexburg. However, the sly bushes do not always berry forth in the same place year after year, so it has become a local festivity to wriggle purpled digits at the supplicating tourist (or neighbor, or close kin) when asked where the treasure hangs this year and fall into a satisfying hush—except for necessary cackles.

The Hushberry Season in Island Park is our only true harvest festival. (Please do not call hunting a "harvest"; it is insulting. I know an elk who does not think he is an asparagus.) The Bugle office gets many interesting questions lobbed through the door (among other things) and so I knew the season was on when someone wanted to know if there was any pectin (for jam) left in town. My mouth watered Pavlovian but, being a slave to your needs, I was busy putting out the newspaper and have had to rely on second-(purpled) hand reports. It is rumored to be one of the finest seasons in years, possibly due to the wet spring and sultry heat.

Yes, I know where they are. So what? It is not always the purpose of journalism to inform. (The tippy-top of Green Canyon Pass, North Antelope Flat Road, and Bootjack Creek above Henrys Lake.)

The rather silly tradition of keeping the bounty's location a secret is one of the ways a small community bonds itself: a "We know things They don't" kind of thing. Religious orders do much the same thing, as do men's clubs. The Fraternal Order of Road-Killed Butter-Squash has a special handshake and secret passwords, I am sure. Perhaps our own Targhee Ladies Club knows things I do not know. I certainly hope so.

But there is a profound difference between something that is an exclusive secret and something that is simply too special to explain or convey easily. High Summer and the berries that crown it are a rite of passage to us who live here all year long. We have seen all the seasons turn in this valley and have not only waited for the deliciously tanged berries, but have worked at being here, making homes here, while we waited. The Hushberry Season is special to us for having paid the entrance dues. All things are special here; the seven months of snow, the wooly-wild storms, the awe of a thin cold winter night with the stars in your lap. But some things are better-special. Think of a snow-cream sundae with a berry on top. It is like that.

Things that are held in common that cannot be explained, that must be experienced together, are the fruit of shared life. A loyalty born of special history, an un-worded fondness, a sense of community, and more...

Last week I sat quietly and watched the dust and heat mingle in her hair. It was not a day that you wished to touch someone, my shirt clung to my back, there was a fine silky film of sweat on the inside of her wrist just above the pulse I watched and timed to my own warm blood. It did not matter that we would not touch in the August mountain heat for there had been too many other things that mattered. Many special moments shared between us that could not be explained, did not need to be explained to each other. While I watched, the low afternoon light caught a place of her, between the ear and the pulse in her throat, and another special moment bore fruit that was our secret.

Perhaps she will bring me Hushberries this season.

DANCING THE MOOSE

O ver the years up here in the mountains I seem to have become a Grizzly Adams on a much smaller scale. Chipmunk Adams, perhaps. Something like that.

Like any red-blooded, manly, chest-haired dreamer and fool, I arrived in Island Park a decade ago with visions of mountain men and rugged ways and conducting life on such a large scale that it would pull me up with it. Our mountains are a grand big place with grand big creatures and I would live among them like Paul Bunyan and use Sawtelle Mountain as a doorstep and Yellowstone for central heating.

For a while it went just fine. I have met the bear and sung with the elk. I have foot-raced the bison and danced with the moose. There have been years with little between me and the winter, and summers spent at the edge of the map. But as large as the stage is and, now, how familiar the players, the years brought more grandeur to the place and less grandiosity to me. These later days there are even rare times when I have nothing to prove; a select few moments when I need not growl or bugle or push to the head of the pack; sometimes whole afternoons when the mountains are— thankfully—too large to conquer or impress with my wonderful self. The finest gift of this place is humility and the best punch line in the Joke Bag is to be notched down enough to find yourself amusing. This year there is no leader of bears or Best of the Herd; there is merely a celibate hermit and his old cat writing weekly love letters and moving over a little in his little place for the flying squirrels and this-year skunks that have come in out of the dusk. Chipmunk Adams, an equal among equals.

Last week I met my early self in Heaven (translation: my newly acquired land which is very high up, nearly impossible to get to, but shockingly pleasant when you get there). I was taking in the evening on the porch area of a very tattered and old tent while listening to the pipsqueek elk blunder around in the Doug firs behind me. Senior elk don't get serious until the ground crusts and the air bites back, so they were lounging around looking impressive with the cows up by treeline. But the junior elk like to thrash around and pipsqueek before the season goes to full rut, so they come out to play and squeek at each other—a tweet, really.

I got up to disturb things and wandered over to a small meadow below a shale cliff where I encountered the moose. Bull moose. Throat swole and all. In season and a mood.

My first rule about being social around large animals is not to make eye contact and the second is to stifle large noises. This time it didn't work—I gawked and let out a huge guffaw, making the situation unpleasant for the moose and tricky for me.

It was like this: moose are sort of prehistoric and gangly looking in the first place. I wasn't up close enough yet for the usual impression that they are also impossibly large and have bad breath. Young male moose, like elk and deer, have antlers, but unlike other ungulates the rack is not in proportion to the body mass. I would guess this example was a two or three year old, which is plenty much of moose, but the spatulate rack looked like it belonged on a medium-sized dog. A silly party hat kind of thing on the big lug. So I hooted and stared at the several hundred pound cartoon.

He seemed to recognize his image problem and puffed up with pretense, shook the pathetic headpiece, and curled a lip to let out a bully snarl—it came out a piddling hiss. I recognized too much of myself years ago (or last week, or yesterday) and convulsed with suck-air laughter. The teenage moose decided then to have a major snit and walk all over several places of me, which was a problem since Heaven is mostly up and down and there are very few spots to run, except off. Off cliffs, for instance.

I tried big bull behaviour rule number three: always travel at ninety degree angles to large angry things bigger than you are. That brought me into a hugging match with a large Doug fir—me peeking around one side and junior having a pubescent fit on the other. Dancing with the moose. Up looked fine, so I did, and the bull finally wandered off somewhere to find some respect.

I went back to find the tent full of flying squirrels—a fine punch line and reminder that you cannot travel very far from yourself. I had not noticed that the area was perfect flying squirrel habitat— broken off stumps with plenty of vacated woodpecker holes—but the squirrels had noticed the peanut butter sandwiches I had brought for dinner.

I had three sandwiches so we shared while watching the lake very far below turn autumn shades of gold in the twilight and the sky move over for stars. The squirrels settled in just like home while the pipsqueeks tweeted out in the dark.

Chipmunk Adams in the Rockies.

PASSION BELOW ZERO

It is my kind of weather: A north wind chirping crisply between the trees and into the unchinked corners of the cabin, a day sky beyond blue, the ground too bright with snow, and a night sky busy with pilgriming stars. Island Park—at least where I live, tucked into an off-edge of the Box Canyon—is neither a comfortable nor convenient place to winter, but it suits me. I was born with a marvelous talent for sloth, and watching frost form on the kneecaps provides for me both motive and movement to be something other than ornamental.

Winter life would be just a hunky-dorry routine of woodheat and books and cat-company and nose-deep-in-the-beard hibernation if it weren't for the sudden storms of passion that come blizzarding out of memory and howling down the veins. The storms visit too often and are too furious to be comfortable, but it is my fault; I have chosen to winter here and not be comfortable and I have chosen not to close my heart to the storms.

It is said that passion is a thing of the tropics; as if humidity and heat somehow loosened up the chemistry. Hogblither. That kind of passion is merely the product of perspiration, too much rum and the incessant whining of too many insects. I have spent some considerable time in the tropics and what passes for passion there is just a temper tantrum to interupt the general lethargy.

Recently, hard against dusk, and under the mountains, I began to listen to one of Wagner's Prelude's as Mars started to rise in the east. You know the piece (they made a marvelous cartoon years ago around the music with Elmer Fudd as Brunhilde and Bugs Bunny in a supporting role), it opens with horns in a major chord swelling with such majesty and slowness that you want to get up and kick the turntable so they will pick up the pace, your pulse running ahead of the deliberate cadence. It is deep forest music, large mountain music, the violins and cellos finally bringing shadows and form to the marching promenade of horns. The wind caught up and grew colder, my mountains thickened and wrapped me, and the stars came out in a chorus. And then, held in the huge harmonies, I remembered her.

Being in love is self-destructive. The high singing mated joys and the low writing forevers of anguish are essential parts of the orchestra. Love at its healthiest is self-destructive because so much of your time, your hope, your self becomes invested in someone and something else. That is good—often painful, like birth, but good. It makes you larger in a way nothing else can. But love unrequited, or less than honest, or orphaned by distance or indifference, or crippled by history, can turn you against yourself and destroy in a hundred petty and terrible ways.

Passion is a huge word meant only for the large places: It means both great suffering and great desire. The mountains will hold such a word, perhaps especially in winter. Stars against the cheek, the wind always coldly near. Fire and ice; a place where the heart needs to warm itself against another needing heart.

The music mused to refrain as Mars rose higher and I laughed in the dark: once during one of those weak, unsure moments I have too often, I had asked what I was to her. You are my quality control, she said. Wrapped in the mountains, I laughed again. Yes, yes. And you so much more for me. I have heard the horns with you often.

Be it well with you, I pray, wherever you are.

AIN'T SHE SWEET

"You look really terrible," she said.

"Geniuses stay up all night and genius around," I snarled. I pulled away from the desk and placed an unsightly hand on my really terrible forehead. "Have I withered beyond hope from my normally drop-dead handsome self?"

"You should take better care of yourself," she honked. Honest. She is very pretty, but she honks.

"I'll apply for a full-body transplant in the morning," I said, looking around the desk for something fatal to throw at her.

She pointed her tongue at me. "There are at least twelve things I don't like about you," she said, turned and flounced off. Ain't she sweet? She flounces very well for someone who honks.

Tis the season to be tolerant. Family that does not flock often at other times of the year, gather at the holidays to pass inspection on each other, but are very civilized about it. Uncle Bozo can get nogged out face down in the mashed potatoes, but that is fine, ha ha, it's just his way, bless him. Any other time of the year he would be put on the first bus to Elsewhere, but it is Christmas and we must tolerate these little faults in each other.

Fortunately I do not make a habit of being civilized, so I can be picky and critical all year long. Even, until just lately, about her.

Out the window the snowflakes were bumping into each other before getting organized into a real howler. It's an interesting relationship: when I first felt my blood jump the banks and head her way, I sat her down and very slowly, in plain english, explained exactly how I felt about her and exactly what I wasn't going to do about it. That seemed better than all right with her, and we settled into this comfortable across-the-room Victorian friendship. I see her once in a while and adore all over her while she does things and ignores being adored. There is a freedom, like in a good marriage, in knowing that you are both looking at the same map, both playing by understood rules.

One of the things I had explained was that while she was a Princess of the Well, and could call out what small music I have, it was not her responsibility, not any of her business. No babysitting, no emotional blackmail. I explained that what I felt doesn't do that, that good love doesn't require or imply obligation. Thank you for the harmonies I could not have fetched without you, but never linger past your own needs—it would demean us both in the end.

She looked at me as if she had always known about all those wise things, but was surprised that I did. Maybe frequent stupidity is one of those twelve things she doesn't like about me. She was being kind, of course, about the twelve things. When she is not too busy being wise, she is kind.

I have never been in love with someone who didn't have things about them I didn't like. Some days the didn't-like stuff would get out of hand and I would forget to remember that I was in love. Those were bad days and there were too many of them. It is often too convenient to butcher love up into only acceptable pieces.

As the mountains started to weather off some of my arrogant pickiness, I began to notice things in stages: one day I noticed that her left elbow, while flawed and lacking some grace, was connected to many other greatly worthy parts. Would I love her all the more if her elbow were altered to turn more pertly? I decided not. I decided I loved her just fine. I then noticed that I didn't need to worry over, or fret, or plot about, the imagined maybe-improved version of her since the in-front-of-me her was doing nicely. It was a relief.

A few blizzards and humilities later, I noticed that I could apply the same principle to her astonishing temper and pig-headed stubborness. I began to stop giving out love in doses and started admiring more often the present-model her.

Finally, after I had been beaten up in the mountains discovering that I really was clumsy and would always be clumsy, I woke up one morning and found that I no longer wanted to be personally involved in altering someone's life—including my own—because they didn't come up to some impossible standard. I decided that she could come through the door and shoot me twelve times with a horse pistol while muttering bad poetry and I would still love her just fine. It's a package deal, you see, and really none of my business to get critical about how I love her.

Even the idea of being 'tolerant' now sounds stupidly patronizing. Either accept what is before you or walk away from it, but don't meddle because you think you know better how things should be. Let it be holiday all year.

The snowflakes finally read the directions and began to pile up on things and cling to the windowpane. I could hear the wind around the door, wanting to come in. I could smell the dark starting in the trees. I went outside and held out my hand, palm up. The snowflakes touched me and vanished. It is hard to hold on to things in the mountains; it's not right, it doesn't work. A piece of last light scattered sudden colors in the snow. It is hard to want what you don't have in the mountains when you are given so much so often.

A half-moon pulled loose from the clouds and I looked at the snow that had now gathered on my boots and in my open hand. This moon is a treasure, I thought, not my treasure, merely its own glorious treasure. But thank you for the light.

1991

It Ain't Right, But It's Fine

Last week I almost drove off the Buffalo River bridge while trying to commit heinous murder. It started like this: this has been a very confusing winter season. Nothing seemed to want to sit still in its proper place and behave. Blizzards and record-boggling cold as 'Rocky Mountain Christmas Presents' are acceptable and timely, since every mountain man book I've read says that's how it's supposed to be. My own personal years in Island Park have seen a few holiday weather patterns like that, especially eight or nine years ago.

This January thaw was right on time, though a little too thawish. February was nonsense and I had to pull out my driver's license every few days to see what state I was in. Then the damn robins started lurking in my yard a few weeks ago, completely discombobulating any remaining sense of the Order Of Things. The cat pranced through the door the other night with a meadow vole, one of those hamster-like rodents that are plenty numerous up here but usually politely out of sight until May or so. The old goof cat was just showing off and took the frightened and confused critter back outside to play with, but it left me confused too. Here I am, a guy who even wrote a calendar this year, and I can't figure out which season it is.

It's been interesting—I use the word in the same context as the old Chinese curse: "May you live in interesting times."

There are two kinds of living things that make a home in or visit Island Park, the tropistic and the notional. The tropistics set their schedules and behaviour by the angle and duration of sunlight, a product of astronomy that has nothing (or very little) to do with the local weather. Eagles are tropistic; they start courtship in late April and get the eggs down between May fifth and ninth every year. Our osprey return, male first, between April eighteenth and twenty-first, every year. Some of our flowers bloom and seed on a daylight-length schedule.

The notionals (my term) on the other hand just stick a nose or beak or tendril into the wind and take a notion to do things by adjusting some very deep genetic and chemical clock based on local conditions. Robins are notionalists, they show up when they think things look good. (I saw one guess wrong in the last week of March 1983 and freeze to death, the earliest until now I have seen one here). The fall rut is notional, moving around in time and duration based on temperature and moonlight. These notional thrill-seekers lead a very interesting life, I'm sure, playing seasonal roulette, the excitement of risk and all. I, however, am a very bull-headed tropistic Taurus, dull as a stump and steady as the stones, and want to get up in the morning, read what my calendar says, and look out my window and find it so.

It has not been so. Back to the near-murder scene:

I was prancing back up the hill last Wednesday afternoon in a truck packed with fresh-printed newspapers when I spotted on the bridge, floozying around in the sunshine, a red-wing blackbird. I admit it, I snapped. A Taurus obsessed by a sense of timely purpose and schedule can only be pushed so far. I swerved to brutally kill the pest. It cawed at me in derision and held its ground. I pulled back from the brink, humiliated, only out of my sense of duty and the fact that I hadn't paid the bills yet that week, something I meant to do if any money happened by the office looking for directions.

Still, it made me feel lousy. Red-wing blackbirds are migratory (and notional) and send scouts up to Island Park to look things over in late April or so. The damn bird belonged here now about as much as this last February belonged in this winter. I didn't pay the bills with the money that wasn't there and went back to the bridge with the office flyswatter, but the pesky bird had migrated to a tall tree across the river. I went home and sulked.

This week things got better, maybe, sort of. I replaced the calendar on the office wall with a season-less picture of Alice in Wonderland, which seemed fitting. The red-wing scouts brought back the rest of the herd and the bridge is now filthy with howling blackbirds. Yesterday a nice blizzard blew in that must have missed the bus last February and, between broken blasts of sunshine, white-outed the highway and dropped a few feet of snow. I stuck my head out the office door into the storm and could hear the blackbird choir skichreeching and carrying on down by the bridge, just like a fine May morning.

I give up.

Problems In Communal Living

The local folk and distant-enough neighbors assume I live alone back here at my end of the road retreat, Hermit's Hovel. Peaceful. Serene. An untroubled middle-aged writer's sanctuary from a frantic world paced by hysteria. Contentment Corner.

Phui, I'm thinking about hiring a traffic cop. Herds of birds mob the porch feeding stations in a cacophany of wing beats and chirp-song. Flocks of squirrels dash around the eaves in play and challenge, turning the old cabin into a furry Merry-Go-Round. As the feeding stations empty from the press of the crowds, things begin to tap at the windows to remind the recluse of his chores and obligations. Mostly chickadees tapping at the sills, but sometimes larger things tapping, drawing longer shadows into the one room, the pale winter light lessened even more. Things go thump in the night out on the porch, thump up in the loft, sometimes under the bed thump, sometimes thumping very often. A growl sometimes. Mr. Hitchcock could have made a movie here. The cat and small bird have learned to ignore it all, the bird snores on the couch while the cat frumps before the fire, their faith held fast in the protecting man. Sometimes the man is not so sure; a scratch at the door, a small rustle in the dark pine outside the window. Too small a moon to show things and sometimes too tiny a courage for the man to go out and thump his chest in the dark.

But more often there are wonderous surprises in all this busyness. Last week in the just-dawn I stepped out for the morning pilgrimage to the outhouse. It is a little of a hike; living in Island Park is patterned by weather and so the placement of the outhouse was decided by prevailing winds and such, but it has a fine view of the aspens and a set of nearly tiny spike antlers nailed over the door to cutesy up the thing and offer some dignity to a plywood temple of very basic utiltity. I moved the cup of tar-pit coffee to the off-hand and opened the door to discover—or rather be announced at—that there was a marten in the Loo.

Pine martens are a beautiful member of the weasel family; pumpkin-orange colored, about the size of an elongated house cat, with Elizabeth Taylor eyes. Perhaps they are also members of the snake family since they hiss, spit, strike, and wouldn't back down from a high-geared hippopotamus. That whole weasel tribe—skunks, badgers—has a mean spirit and a truly astonishing ferocity. One member inspired my favorite quote from an old trapper: "Wolverines endangered? I sincerely hope so!"

I pushed the door back quickly and fell in the snow laughing, slinging coffee around. There were obvious problems: the out-house is a one-holer and the marten had taken the high-ground on the hatch. I prefer not to be fanged by wild animals while at my morning hygenic privacies. I had caught sight of the beginnings of a nest in the corner (they build round stick nests like magpies or ouzels) so it might be a long campaign. I was dressed in my usual morning outhouse-sprint uniform of knee-boots, coffee cup and nothing else, and was now sitting in the snow with the giggles, lis-tening to an occasional hiss and bark from behind the door. Gastro-intestinal urgency finally compelled me to kick snow away from Emergency Bush # 3. As I write this, the marten is still there. It is not hard to tell; martens are not subtle.

The squatter marten is not an isolated incident of life at the Hovel. Years ago this same small cabin was on another property at the southern end of Island Park. In the first year I made the acquaintance of a pubescent bull moose that had claimed the same property. After some initial snorts and posturing (on both our parts), we settled into a comfortable four-year relationship of tolerance. Though I never offered to stroke his nose or pat him on the rump, we could pass a very few feet from each other without raising any hackles (on both our parts) as long as eye contact was avoided.

He developed the habit of coming up from the river after his evening graze and sleeping behind the Hovel where it was dark, away from the road and against the forest. I learned this since that property's Bush # 3 was in the same area, prevailing winds and such. The insulation was (and is) lousy in the little cabin, so as the autumn nights cooled down into the full winter cold, the moose took to leaning against the back wall to sleep—for the cabin-glow warmth, I think. The pattern developed in late winter of the first year until I could anticipate the soft thump on the wall an hour after twilight, just as the serious owl hooting started deep back in the pines. By the fourth year the moose had grown hugely into mature bull-ness but our relationship, and the pattern, had not changed. The thump had become a major thud as he moosed the back wall, rocking the small cabin on its piers and swaying the ceiling lantern. But by then the thump was a welcome household sound, the cat never opening an eye, like the slamming of the door when a family member had come safely home.

The moose left that next summer. Whether he was taken in a hunt or had just taken one of those wandering notions that moose are fond of, I don't know. I do know that I miss that thump in the night and still find myself listening for it on quiet, star-bright evenings when I am tired and the world seems a touch less old.

THE SEASON OF THE HAG

Poor dear mountain. Poor bedraggled unkept Rockies. Spring, as a visual experience, is not very kind to my forest home. The other stage-settings of the year are famous for their alure. Summer (with water) is verdant and rich-ripe, a banquet of color and surging, unsophisticated lifeness. Autumn is crisp and golden, the poet's season in the mountains. Winter is pristine and naked majesty. But spring here is a plain and dull child, muddy and nasal and sometimes—unless you go up very high and very away—embarrassingly ugly.

The famous Springtime in the Rockies is an old and common fiction, swooned over by writers in other places at other times, and by sly photographers who peddle tricks and trinkets of light and water into flashy calendars and coffee table books. We who live in Island Park know that the kind of spring oogled over by city poets is really only fifteen minutes long here in our mountains. There is one magnificent day where there *is* a marvelous piece of the hour when the mud has calmed, the snowbanks have turned to lumps sugar-crystal in the sunlight, and a small flashing thread of water works its way between the violets and new ferns, dancing like a fairy tale down to the Henrys Fork River, trout lillies nodding cheerfully on the bank. There are tiny golden dragonflies on the blue violets, only the blue violets not the yellow ones, during that hour. Then, in a puff of sudden heat and dust and running mud, our spring is gone; out come the large dull brown dragonflies and the (it seems) even larger hunger-cruising mosquitoes. It is probably a good thing that this kind of magic is sudden and brief, for I have seen our true spring several times and the beauty would be unbearable if beheld too long.

The few weeks called 'spring' are awkward for my mountain; mud turned ditch-rut greasy, dirty snow thrown like old rags between the trees, the trees still brown in their dry sleep. Mountain as hag. The season of the hag, sung of by poets and painters not here, but in truth an awkward orphan of a clumsy time.

In this Year of Two Winters in Island Park I was amused in my frustrations by an image summoned by the storm(s) last week:

My woodpile near the door of Lesser Frogpond was becoming a spring island just a few weeks ago; the snow backing up and off, small brownish havens of dirt peeping out near the logs. This week I necked around the door and the pile was gone, a mere lump of white in a greater sea of white. The stove was also empty and the old cat cranky with cold, so I set forth. About the third belt-high snowdrift I remembered it was, after all, March and perhaps I should fix this mountain plenty of coffee and make soft cooing noises for a few days (or weeks) lest it bite my head off while it was trying to wake up. These mountains are like that, you know, moody and complex, sullen and grand. I have had mornings myself like the spring my mountain is trying to wake up to this year. On the way back with the (wet) wood, the cat tapping a paw impatiently at the cabin door, another image came:

Once upon a life ago, a cherished friend came to this cabin door in this season. I opened the door at the knock and she stood a little aside out of the storm, wet clear through to her heart, her hair clasped to head and shoulders like sodden bark, mud to the knees, her skin in the failing light the color of pale sleeping watercress. She had returned and I thought I had never seen anything so lovely as her. I opened my arms and welcomed her into the fire and myself.

I have learned to see my mountain in these weeks of spring season in much the same way. The mountain is coming in from winter, all ungainly and ugly and damp—all endearingly, awkwardly lovely in its return. Welcome and waking and loved as it comes home from the cold.

ASKEW

I have never been one of those people who could chew gum and walk at the same time, so the other morning was something of a problem: too near me at the end of the counter was a Self Important Person in full prattle, drowning out whatever thoughts might stop by in my head for a chat. I was trying to get enough coffee in me to flee, and at the same time curl my earlobes up into the ear channels to block out this boor's imitation of a sandhill crane in rut. I finally convinced one leg to wake up enough for a hobbling retreat. I do not mind folks talking to themselves, I do it often myself, but I become offended if they insist that I listen.

Back at my cabin, Grumps Getaway, I pondered people who lean hard on the world around them. I spent the first forty years of my life trying to get noticed and was always surprised and insulted when I was noticed for all the wrong reasons. All I was requesting was absolute, complete adoration and loyalty; instead, in the early years, some of my students found me merely amusing (I was always afraid to ask why) and some friends seemed more affectionate as the distance increased.

Obviously we all have a problem, now and again, with persona versus personality, when our presentation does not quite match up with what we think we are. I have presented an obviously adorable cast and float to too many sneering trout. It is like that.

I think I have been looking askew at the presentation of self too long. This minor revelation came on the evening of ponder mentioned above. The animals were being too animal in the likes of two-year-olds, interupting my ponderousness, so I had plopped the bird into its cage on the floor and set food for the cat next to it. While I was gumming the dried bread crumbs and stale water that we hermits eat, the bird snaked its head out through the bars (which she could probably walk between) and pilfered some tuna fish from the cat bowl. The cat found this almost funny and moved his face, teeth first, against the cage. The bird found that rude and pecked the cat in the nose. I swallowed some more mold and green water, watching the negotiating process.

Quite suddenly a brain cell fired and I looked more carefully at the bird. She obviously thought that the cage was not there to keep her in—it was there to keep us out. Many of the social displays of self—our persona—are there for the same reasons; to keep others out. The loud boor at the counter would probably have fled in terror if I had slithered over and started making psychiatrist noises. Instead, she had erected a wall of words that kept anyone else from getting too close. A little neurotic perhaps, but we have all at times been too noticible publically to keep from being too noticed personally. Self-erected barriers.

The bird got hold of the cat's tail, which he had placed carefully close to the cage, and I had to terrify them both with threats of spanking. I looked out the window of the cabin wall that was there to keep the winter out and noticed that the lowering sunshine was still warm enough to melt snow on the woodpile. A pair of robins hop-scotched under the nearest pine. The moon was coming up March-high, spring-orbit. I scratched at my mood and knew that when the stars came out the constellations would have leaned farther west than my attitude. I pulled the blanket down from the door, opened the door, and left the door open.

The cabin fever had finally broken.

No Bird Is An Island

One evening last week, just after the squirrel had come into the cabin and stolen my toothbrush for the second time that day, a friend and his family arrived at the door with two recently-egg killdeer they had rescued from some juvenile terrorists in Last Chance, each tiny bird no larger than one of my thumbs. I patted my friends children and made soothing noises and sent them on their way, the little pieces of feet and fluff nested in my hand, but of course it was hopeless.

Over the years I have dealt with hawks and owls and moose and such—big sturdy beasts you could pry open the beak or snout on and shovel things in—but these bitsy birdlets made me feel huge and gross and useless, the thin pointed beaks designed for eating bugs smaller than I could even see. Killdeers are members of the precocial group of birds, meaning that like chickens and pheasants and ducks, they hatch wide-eyed and ready to run. I wasn't too worried about feeding them just yet; these young birds internalize the remaining yolk sac before hatching and are able to go without eating for as much as two days. They do need to be kept warm and dry though, so that first night the old cat (he has been through this before) and I took turns with the pair; a somewhat uncomfortable experience since they call to each other constantly and like to brood by shoving their sharp beaks up under the chest hairs on both man and cat.

They were alive come morning—to my surprise—but very weak, one much more so than the other. By the end of the day I despaired of trying to get some food in them. Even eyedroppers and tweezers were too big and I much too clumsy to poke insects or worms down them. Finally in desperation I sucked some strained beef baby food into a very small straw, grabbed them each by the lower beak, placed the food end of the straw in the corner of the now-open hole, and blew the food straight into them. Brutal, but it worked and though one was still much smaller and weaker than the other, they both began to run around on the cabin floor following the late afternoon sunshine.

The next morning they were still alive. Remarkable. I placed the birds on the floor to let the warm sunshine brood them, left instructions with the cat, and went down the road to the KOA for the daily shower, pulling the door behind me. (The cabin is tilted slightly so that the door swings against the jamb, allowing the cat to pull open the door when he wishes and shoulder his way back in). When I returned the sun had moved around so that there was no warm light on the floor—and no birds. After a quick search of the small cabin I cursed out the old cat roundly; though he has never done so with birds we have cared for, I was certain he had eaten them. Later, I went out to fetch something from the truck and nearly stepped on the two killdeer scrunched down in the sunshine at the edge of the cabin. Apparently the cat had noticed them get chilled when the sun had moved off and took them each outside, out of the wind, in his mouth I suppose, pawing open the door each time. There was no wind that day to blow open the door, and it was closed when I had returned. I apologized sincerely and often to him, and even left the birds outside since the stronger one had taken to feeding himself on bark bugs and running brightly about. I went out and found them later by listening for their calls to each other.

That evening, finally, the weaker one began to fail; pneumonia, I think. It often takes the young weak ones. I stayed up the night dripping bird antibiotics into it, one tiny drop each hour, but just as the sun was rising the killdeer rolled over in my hand and died.

The sibling bird, who seemed very robust and healthy, came over and looked in my hand, calling over and over again. The cat looked at me and went to the door, pawed it open and left. He and I knew what would happen: About twenty minutes later the surviving killdeer stopped calling and began to sag. It died about noon, for all of my efforts. I know what it died of, but I quite honestly do not have the words to explain it.

Loneliness, emptiness, dislocation, and alienation are not just conditions of being human, they are common to all who have the gift of being alive. We are all not just connected—we need to be connected. There is an old Chinese story: Hu Shi was a famous lute player in ancient times. His good friend Chan could play no instrument, but would often listen intently to Hu play his lute in the evenings when just the two of them were alone in the palace garden. After many years of garden evenings, Chan died. Hu Shi cut the strings of his lute with a sword and, though he lived another thirty years, never played again.

Precocial birds like the killdeer also play for each other. Though the eggs are obviously laid at different times, they all hatch out together for obvious reasons of survival. They accomplish this by making clicking noises to each other, in the egg, in the nest, the eggs touching, a week or so before hatching. Like a little ragtime band, they all get tuned to each other, the older ones slowing their growth, the younger accelerating, until they all hatch in harmony, connected to each other in ways necessary and vital. Like Hu the player and Chan the listener, like the cat and I perhaps, like some older much-loving married couples I have known.

The one killdeer died of being frail, the other died of being lost. I hope I can remember that, and be a little kinder to those near me.

The Beginning

End Of The Season Sale!
Close Out on Crowds!
Half Off on Highway Space!
Big Reductions on Rudeness!
All Remaining Fish On Sale (no returns, please)!
Special Today on Solitude!

Labor Day has been the traditional end of the busy season in Island Park for several generations. The visitors flow out of the mountains like spring snowmelt, taking with them the things we here share so well: dreams and fantasies and memories of fish and full-vision vistas that fill the heart. We wish them well, these high-summer drifters and, perhaps just a little, we wish them gone. There always, every year, seem to be so many of them, as if the valley had become a seasonal tempest lake, brimmed off to the edges with fun-goers and busy voices. Most are very nice and some are genuinely interesting brief companions. A few every year stay here in Island Park, siren-songed into the mountains to make a life for a while. But there are so many of them.

Maybe the problem for those of us who home here is the so sudden tumble from the valley's peaceful winter, so thin of people, to the rip-tide swarm of summer visitors. Few of those visitors who ten-fold our population on Memorial Day realize that we homefolk are just a few days shy of snow-choked roads and brisk trips to the woodpile. Springtime in the Rockies is a fancy, a fast swing tune lasting a week or less, mostly less. Summer for us is more shell-shock than sunshine and arrives, like the tourists, much too quickly to be easy. But after this weekend that will be over, and it will come fall.

Autumn is for us. Autumn is long on beauty here. We will begin to plow seriously on to Thanksgiving, go into full winter tuck, but it is a long wonderful time until then. Berries and grouse and big hopper-mad fish and howling elk and slow walks in the gold trees, the season in Island Park is just beginning. Gathering bush-fruit, gathering the winter wood, gathering back the sensibilities dulled from summer that make us cherish these mountains.

Fall is my favorite of the times here. Winter is very fine too, but the soul breathes slowly then, the passions nesting quietly. Autumn is very alive and mature and rich, and I have always felt most whole then, most vital and awake. Last week was the full moon and, harvest-bright high, it shared the night with a small low lightning storm in the east. I watched a friend turn slowly in the water, the water running from her hair moonwhite down her back and into the pool as dark as the sky. All in context, I thought. She is as beautiful now as then, but framed in the moonlight of fall she was as beautiful as my heart could let her be.

The poets say spring is for love and perhaps it is so, for the very young or those that would dream they are. After all, that spring-such love is peddled by Cupid, that pudgy cherub of no years. But there in the high moon and thunder I thought of the older one, Pan, playing his pale pipes by the night-calm river, watching the sprites bathe in silvered shadow, their laughter calling across the water to his old knowing heart.

Only in autumn, with a choir of elk up the mountain and the visitors gone off, can passion grow rich enough to harvest.

AN ECHO IN THE FOREST

This Sunday before last, I crawled out of the cabin loft in the wee-dawn to find the old cat prancing a grouse around the room that he had brought in to toy with. In a decade of being partnered to this cat he has brought in many a beast to show off but never, in all those years of living with house-bound hawks and owls and whatever, has he brought home a grouse. I shooed the bird out with a fluster and peered at the calendar through the thin coming light—it was the opening day of grouse season in Island Park.

I wish the cat wouldn't do things like that; it bullies me off whatever secure mental platform I have perched myself on that day and makes me rethink—again—all my assumptions about what's really going on around me. There is no safety of thought in this magic place, no place to go where you may take things for granted and rest in the security of your illusions. A life lived out in the mountains is a life on the frontier of emotions and ideas, a life of much fun but tolerant of few old prejudices.

Cats read calendars maybe, bears find almost empty bean cans and—much as I would—pick up a flat stick and spoon the remaining goodies out. I once had a hawk guest who carried a small teddy bear everywhere with him. I have seen a swan fight off a grown eagle over the body of her mate. There is a well-mannered pack rat in my cabin now who understands my daily patterns and schedules better than I do myself. There was summer this year in February.

I was not taught that this was the way things are: that all things play—even weather. That all things are good and smart and sometimes even wise at what they are, and can recognize those things even in others not of their own kind; that all things healthy and happy—mouse, aspen, hermit, moose—share a common alertness. They are not just wary or frightened, but alert and responsive to not being alone.

I think it is like this: reality is interactive and playful. To have fun and be strong you must learn to respond and not just react to the whirling vibrant other-life going on around you. (If someone whams your knee and your leg jerks, you are reacting; if you notice the whammer first and move your knee, you are responding.) Life conducted that way is resonant. It is impossible to be in love alone, for instance; you must be loved also or you are feeling something else. All your assumptions and expectations about cause and effect must come Humpty Dumpty down before you can happily come out to play. Then cats who fetch grouse on opening day and bears that ponder out things and our postcard days that leapfrog seasons, all will make perfect sense. Alice in Wonderland did her research in Island Park.

I saw her for a few moments last week and wondered at the unspoken resonance I felt. Pulse skipped up an octave and stayed there, nerve endings moved out to the edges like evening deer coming out from treeline to feed. My breath adjusted to the faint beat I could see in her neck just below her ear. I have seen animals in our forest do this thing, this awareness of each for the other, this dance without movement, song without words. It is not merely flesh and the gush-driven chemistry of sex, it is life acknowledging life. I know you are here, says this thing. We are alert and we are here.

There is a place out Chick Creek Road where Echo—that poor orphan of the lesser Greek gods—lives. You must go to the edge of our volcano and then go steeply up where the younger Yellowstone caldera has leaned on us and pushed up the country like folds in a blanket shoved to the foot of a summer-hot bed. There is a canyon there, drained by Split Creek, at the edge of the North Fork Fire, where you may capture the resonance of things.

I went there between the storms so that the wind would not challenge my message and began to explain about her down into the stones and distant falling water. The things she could not hear began to come back to the cliff edge, and I altered my speech to a cadence with the echo and then a chant: a poem as ancient as the elk howling somewhere behind me on the folded ridges.

All life is resonant, all things well and strong respond. I felt the mountain move ever so slightly from the booming echos and chant and, satisfied, I moved away from the edge and went home.

CALL OF THE WILD

I saw another of the faces of God last week—not a difficult thing to do if you live in Island Park and stay awake to things. This time I was pulled awake a little after one in the morning, thrown out of slumber into that deep-night kind of clarity that meant I had been listening to something at the edge of my dreams.

Out the window in the dark, the elk had been calling for a little over a week. It had started with the pathetic junior tweets of the young bulls not yet come of age and chorused in the last few days to the high silver whine-bugle of the big males claiming ground and courting rights. I moved to the window and listened to the howls and grunts coming from Antelope Park a little over a mile away and then realized what had called me awake: every so often there was a lower, louder, longer grunt, like the sounding of a deep temple drum, and it was on my side of the river, up the canyon. I looked out to treeline; the moon was swollen near full, light enough to see, light enough to go.

I do not know what would possess a man over forty to leave his warmed bed in the deepest night and go out to run with the elk under the trees. There were some health problems the last few years—over with just these last weeks—and perhaps life returned feels called to take part in one of life's high dramas. Whatever. I pushed the cat down deeper in the bag and kick-started the old soft boots and went.

I followed the moon up the river, until I could hear him crashing the brush as well as calling, and stepped off the trail to roll in the yarrow and mint weeds to take the man stink off. I needn't have bothered; I found him by the smell of the season, his musk pushed out by his own heat into a crisp windless night, in a clearing ringed with aspen in the moonlight.

I dropped to one knee, mostly out of awe, and whispered myself into a stand of tiny pines. He looked like a damn Clydesdale with antlers, easily the largest bull elk I have ever seen, the neck swollen into a pulsing bag, eyes plainly fever-red to me even at the yards that separated us. And he roared. Roared between calls while he horned up the soil and berry branches and threw them out into the dark. I gaped. I have been in these my mountains many years and seen many things but I gaped, jaw slung against my chest, tongue dashing at the teeth.

He stopped and listened to the calls across the river, antlers pointed at the moon, and then sang—a call so ancient and pure of motive that I recognized it in my blood and felt my hair stand. I put my hand flat on the cold dirt and could feel the great roar that followed the bugle tremble up my arm and fall inside.

Like a ballet, the cows moved ghost-soft at the edge of the clearing, some coming very near me as I hung kneeling in the dark. No, not a ballet. The bull roared again and chopped at the night. Like an opera, like the Wagner opera Tannhaeuser, where the horns ride you so high that you must see the great dark trees soaring and run with the long legs antlered of the close forest.

Two of the moon-white cows glided near me and the lathered beast, who knew I was there, turned his red eyes at me and growled. Growled, I swear, like the sound of two boulders rolling together. I stood up and stepped back, the cows moving off slightly, their eyes bright and watching from the trees. Though it was barely twenty degrees, a fine sweat broke out over all of me. We looked at each other, the cows dancing in the moonlight, and my blood began to warm wild to a boil and I feared that if I did not leave now I would never be able to go home again. The bull snorted and raised his head to challenge his voice out over the river again and I thought: you fool. You fool, you are home.

I clapped my hands twice in the fashion of the orientals complimenting their gods, turned just as the moon was setting gold through the aspens, and walked back down the river to the cabin.

COLORS

Age comes as a surprise to most of us. I don't think the shock is merely the collision of reality with vanity; it is also that we are so intimately, constantly involved with the vehicle that gets old that we do not notice always the small accumulations of prices that must be paid to enjoy another day or week or year.

The other day I came upon someone I had not seen since early spring and she let her lip loose long enough to notice that I was much more grey than she remembered. Har, har, I said, pulling some of the paunch up into the manly-chest regions. Earned every one of those hairs, said I. Dignified looking, she said. You bet, I said.

My male ego and I rushed off to find a Mirror, Mirror on the Wall. It was true, I whined, pawing at my beard. There were at least eighteen more grey hairs. A herd of old hairs. A plague of visited hairs. I've been needing some stronger reading half-glasses too, I thought. And I'd been forgetting things, I remembered. Come to think of it, that left knee has been cranky lately. Woe.

Everything—every place and person, every emotion—has seasons. Everyone agrees right now that autumn in the Rockies is the most beautiful of seasons (everyone, after winter, thinks spring is the best of all; but you know how it is). Autumn is a fine and graceful turning of the summered year from fullness and seeded, winged transport into winter. The summer blooms too hard, too urgently into maturity and so, before life can consume itself like a shooting star, autumn slows and shortens the days into ripeness and full-feathered thought. Haste becomes reflection and, if done gracefully, that becomes wisdom.

As for the year, so for the man. The analogies between human life and the turning of the year are numerous. But I, examining another grey hair I had missed, cry foul. If there is 'Old Man Winter', then why not 'Middle-Aged Autumn'? Golden, glorious autumn so beloved of the poets never got tagged up with a set of years for a man. Fine people from Louis Lamour to Confucius never achieved full burn until after forty, but no one wants to talk lovingly of the age except for a few motivational hysterics who insist on shrieking that Forty is Fun, Life Begins at Forty, and so on. Have a care—those people protesteth too much, I think. I am here, sitting fortyish, and it is fine; I'm just trying to recall if anyone has ever written sonnets to middle-age, as I have to aspen in October.

I am 43, with most of those years having been ridden hard and hung up wet. I do not know if I look good for 43—*there's another damn hair, damn it*—because I do not know what a good 43 is supposed to look like. The cat, who is fifty-ish in people years, doesn't seem to mind how I look. Since he is my only significant relationship, I suppose I should be content (*another hair*). So why do I have this uneasy feeling that there is something wrong?

A few years ago I gave up taking my cues from people (including myself) since I found them (including myself) to be too much a sour stew of moods, mangled motives and misplaced hopes. So this night I left the hovel and took out to see how the forest was handling the middle-age of autumn.

Age comes as a surprise to most of us and, looked at through that end of the telescope, perhaps the home mountain is not coping with its autumn any better than I am with mine. Back in the Box Canyon, among the Doug firs, there is an owl who seems to have forevered along that fast water. Owls live to be about as old as us, sixty years or so. This night, under a furry, frosting moon, I thought he looked cold. Looking closer, I saw him fluffed up, the yellow eyes half closed. He was cold. I could hear hurried whiskers brushing dry grass out in the meadow as the Small Ones chased seed to pile up against the winter. The older trees, robbed of summer's supple sap, creaked in the breeze. Dry leaf rasped against dry leaf. Going home I saw the flying squirrel move slowly across the porch. He is at least three years old that I know of, late middle-age for one of his kind. Maybe he has squirrel-arthritis on these nights.

Perhaps autumn is not as graceful as the poets insist on singing. Perhaps the foreknowledge of winter and the longing remembrance of summer is not easy for any of us; man and tree and squirrel. 'Go not gentle into that night' sang Dylan Thomas, and none of us do. Even the pumpkin vine and the owl get cold as the sap and the blood slow with season and age.

I went in and sat nearer the stove, put a hand on the old cat, and thought that my biggest regret was that, instead of grey, I could not turn gold in this season like my beloved aspen.

TRACKING WELL

Sometimes out in the forest it's tough to tell if you've accidently burgled someone's home. It seems like everything has territory, temporary or fixed, that it doesn't want violated and will chew on the intruder to make its rights known. Over the years I have been bitten by a zoology of things; almost always because I was in the wrong place or had arrived at the unseen doorstep at an inconvenient time.

Just a night last week I was skulking in a thornbush watching an elk contest, when a spider of near-tarantula size dropped on the back of my neck and hove to at my jugular. I swacked at the homeowner brute, with apologies, who plopped off into the dark while I got thorned by the bush—the thorns being the bush version of a moat, I suppose. The elk stopped arguing long enough to bray at me while I slipped back down the trail to find some neutral territory. Once upon an ago in college, I saw a time-lapse film of a single stone where some moss was pushing nasty chemicals ahead of it to drive back invading lichen. Maybe if you sat still long enough against a live pine the thing would grow out and get you. I'm glad my uninsulated cabin won't support house plants; they might rise up some night and evict me.

On the other hand, politeness and good manners out in the woods can save you from needless conflict. All you need to know is who is there and why and where they are. That means you need to be able to read sign, to track, to tell by hoof or snort or musked grasses whether you are in the way or uninvited. Etiquette in the trees is very simple to learn and pleasingly direct, not like the sloppy manners of human society where if you are inelegant the folks will gossip you down. In our mountains if you become rude many of the local inhabitants will just kill you. Learn to track.

I thought I knew how to track, but a few weeks ago I obtained a new pair of eye-glasses (my first) that renewed the landscape for me after nearly a year of being a little short on sight. I am sure that seeing the forest newly again, like so many things, changed me enough to drop a lot of the presumptions about what I was looking at.

Most importantly, I discovered I had been tracking wrong all these years: I had been out looking for, instead of looking. I would go fro with the high calibre camera in hand, looking for elk tracks, and miss the soft bear print snugged in the grass at the edge of the trail. Sometimes that meant a bear-surprise (always a little ticklish), and sometimes that just meant not seeing the bear. I was out looking for something instead of looking plainly at what was there.

I told a young woman recently that you cannot compromise facts and did not realize till much later that I had lied horribly. Of course you can compromise facts. I have done it often by looking for something and thereby missing what was before me because it was not what I thought I was seeking. I have missed seeing the bear too often.

There are men who have come to Island Park to find fish who have missed having the comfort and society of squirrels. This week there will be an army tracking our elk out on mountains splendid with aspen and tiny quick songbirds, the valley slopes cluttered with bright fall berries and small-water springs. I hope the hunters see them too. I have often gone hunting passion in this forest and missed seeing the companion at the edge of the meadow, but with my new glasses I hope to begin tracking well.

JUST TREES

I had thought it was going to be poor harvest of a day, the wind having turned mean and moody, catching the edges of the valley walls and pulling their sharp sting down, wicking all the little joys out of the morning, and turning my head away against the chill. I morosed around the office, pushing papers aside and wanting things I didn't have. Sour wind, sour grapes.

She arrived un-looked for—but it happens like that often—and I went to work while she flounced down and picked up an old copy of the paper, turning to my column and tuning up the quality quiet between us.

I have known her awhile now and was bemused to watch the lips in her brain move while she read. She knows how I write the stuff: as if it were to be spoken, a tiny bouncing ball between the heart and the throat tapping out the words, the cadence helping the meaning along, lyrics sometimes I hope. Out of the edge of my eye I saw her lips move to her mouth and smile about halfway down the page. Finally she un-flounced out of the chair, wished me a good day—which it now was—and left.

I threw a leash on what I was working at and went over to the newspaper to find the spot that had captured her smile. She is a piece of work that one: it was a paragraph describing aspen. A straight-ahead and plain telling of how they looked and acted on an early summer day all fresh-greened and glowing. Not the spot a few lines up of high philosophy, or the silly rant a paragraph away. Not the pompous chatter I too often sink into, or the parlor tricks of word-craft I take such secret delight in. Just aspen on a nice day, what I saw, what we all see who are so fortunate to live here. Just the plain truth of a summer moment. Just trees. I like that lady a lot; she is a ground-wire to my pretense. Just trees.

I listened to a man the other day tell me that things are not what they seem to be, and that somebody (him, apparently) needed to explain what's really going on. I had stopped listening after a while, watching the breeze play tag with a fallen carpet of aspen leaves, so I can't remember if Things were really a UFO conspiracy, the Damn Democrats, secret plots of (now) secret communists, or what. The theme though was that everything was different and more important, in sly ways, than we all thought it was.

I found myself offended, maybe even insulted, but I had to get away from the sot to figure out why. I went out and stood in the dancing leaves and chewed it over. It came finally: how dare this clod decide the world was not good enough the way it was and so had to be something else? I looked down at the leaves nipping at my ankles; they seemed important and just fine at being leaves, no aliens pulling strings here. The breeze was turning in for the night, the sun low over Thurmon Ridge pulling evening after it. I do not think this reality is so impoverished that I need to force-feed it meaning to keep it vibrant and alive. I do not think that what has been put before me is such poor fare that I need to whine it up to a better, though hidden, feast. I looked out at the Just Trees laying a blanket of shadows over the meadow.

I do not need to strain to believe in magic, it is here before me always, in this place, in my home. The friends and the soil and the heart of this place do not need to conspire or hide their meaning and importance. I have been lost enough to think I needed these things explained to me before, only to discover the mountains in my lap were all the meaning I needed or could handle. Sometimes it takes stubbing my toe on a pretty lady's smile to remember that, but I shall try.

BAD TIMING

New Year? Wait a minute! (or a month!!), we're not quite ready up here yet. There's twelve hunnert and forty feet of snow crowding the south wall and more on the way. I'm mostly asleep most of the time and plan on getting more so what with February the Foul around the corner and all. There's nothing blooming and very little biting. The bears are asleep and the Wild Indians pacified. I heard Mt. Sawtelle snore the other night and even the Music of the Spheres has turned into a lullaby. I can't even jump-start the snowshoes in this cold, much less anything that might carry me into a New Year. Communism's history and so am I. It was hard work, leave me alone.

Having a New Year in January in the mountains is about as unfair as having Tax Time in Island Park be the middle of April; no one has any money here in April, we're all chewing hides by that time and eyeing the fat little winter pups to see if the kids would miss one or two. And January is not a practical time to be getting gushy and enthused about a New Year for us; new beginnings, bright resolutions, fancy-fresh dreams are not something we cleave to in January; we cleave to wondering where and what's left of the woodpile, how far and deep it is to the outhouse, how far it is to May. We cleave to a Long Winter's Nap and cleave to each other on the colder long nights. Nothing begins except blizzards in Island Park in January. It's just not fair.

The old cat and I will eve in the New Year as always, with each other, down home in Lesser Frogpond, the stove turned up and the lamps turned down; the way things are supposed to be in the mountains during deep winter. It is a quiet time. No eve on the town. Since I don't drink anymore my tavern-mates would just get smarter while I got dumber as the night wore on, so we (the cat got too old to drink too) just nest in and leave the cheer to others more competent at such things.

We usually don't get stirring with enthusiasm around here until the real Island Park new year shows up: buttercup time, the first croakings of sandhill cranes out in the meadow, around my birthday in May when you first hear the trout whispering to each other, frisking after the bank-side snowflies, planning strategies for the coming season.

This coming New Year I shall become forty-five years old, something I didn't discover until the other night when I was scowling at a calendar while trying to wish Februarys away. My male ego went into something like sticker shock at the knowledge since I was sure I was still eighteen just a few weeks ago. You must understand that the male ego is a delicate little thing, prone to harm, and I had been able to skate around turning forty by noting all the very young fortyish people I had seen in magazines and things, and how yuppie-fresh my whole age group was; after all, Peter Pan was still winging strong at eight-three so I was still a font of virility and manhood. But forty-five? Forty-five is old. I knew so when I was twenty, that forty-five was old, and knew then that I would never be that. I was in shock. Say it ain't so.

The cat (who is sixty-something) was not amused and fanged a request for more wood on the fire for our collective lumbagos, and less whining under the blankets. After a while we both got the giggles over the whole thing; considering the alternative, forty-five will do just fine.

I was so entertained by my self (hermits get this way) that I fetched the story one fine afternoon over to the cabin of someone who used (until then) to be fond of me. While howling over my trauma about becoming 45, I had completely misplaced the fact that she was born in the same year as my self. I rapidly found myself on the step, on the cold side of a closed door, in a hard wind. She doesn't have a male ego, so I wonder why she didn't see the humor of it all. They're funny in January sometimes.

1992

ECLIPSE

I suppose there have always been very human beings around and it just took mileage and years and a place to stand for me to recognize them. I'm pretty good at very grizzly bears and loud autumn elk, and I've always done well with very good books and full poem moons, but very human beings went mostly unnoticed by me until the recent years.

It is dark in Island Park at this time of the winter. Dark most of the time. Fifteen hours of dark in the day, and the days are often thin of sunlight, the light low and dissolved in the winter clouds up this high. Like the light in a room with drawn lace curtains, like the light at the edge of shadows. Last Saturday we had an eclipse, a half-eclipse really, on a cloudy day in Island Park about a half hour before sunset. I had known of its coming, trying to be up on such things, but had forgotten while being muddled in the winter chores. I was splitting the night wood in Lesser Frogpond when the birds quietly left their bread and seed and folded into the treeline. I looked up, suddenly uncomfortable, being used to their ryhthms and patterns, feeling somehow wrong. Then the shadows ran, not crept, away, and I remembered the eclipse was beginning and turned back to the wood. But for a very human moment before the fact intruded, I had heard my heart whisper: No, not yet. There has not been enough light. Not the dark now. No, not yet.

Twenty-one years ago, on the other side of the planet, I had stood up with the rest of the tall dark-skinned people of the village at the beginning of an eclipse and shouted at the sudden dark. They banged pots and shells and fired old muskets and I pulled out bells from my robe and rang them with both hands at the shadows. And, after a time, the dark went away.

I have been taught and told since a child that man is a social creature, that we are civilized because of and by each other. I wandered the fringes of us early, studied us in groups as a profession, and eventually soured just a little on what I discovered in those groups: the hypocrisy too often in me and us that can make so much of socializing unvaluable. The animals, I thought, the animals have a better dignity, a more honest and direct way. If the bear cannot tolerate you it will reach out quickly and kill you, it will not gossip or lie you to death, I thought. And so I sought the society of bears in this place where they live and so few of us do.

I should have been more fair back then, but then the young are rarely fair when they are so busily shaping themselves. To be very human is not just to be very near many of each other. There is more, much more to us, and I had even seen it during the eclipse so many years ago and not been puzzled enough to try to understand it. Among the small tribe in the tiny village there was a quick-bright little old man who I had come to respect, and who stood near me as the dark came. I had made drawings in the dirt for him and showed him how the sun and moon and earth would be, had showed him an almanac a month before and told him when and how long the dragon would swallow the sun. Yes, yes, he said, he had heard of these things and was called wise here in his place and had freed himself from these superstitions. He flipped his hand over and grinned out of his dark small face. When the dark came and I chased the dragon away with my bells and shrieks, I looked over to him and saw his face alive with wonder at the wave-shadows flowing over the ground, sometimes lifting his eyes and clay pot up to shade the failing sky. Others were enjoying the ritual and a few were even quietly afraid, but this man – so old that he must have seen tens of eclipses in his years – was in awe. Transport. Not afraid, not directing the rite as a leader of his people, but overcome with wonder. I knew him well and saw myth and legend and the tales by the fire become real for him, a very human being of complex and elegant receptors, washed in rapture by something so far away.

This week I set the wood aside for a moment and looked up and out. I could not see the eclipse but I could feel it. The birds, my wonderful chickadees, had gone into the pines and would sleep until the light returned. They are wonderful at what they do, but they cannot travel through time like we can. They will remember the seed come morning, but they cannot dream our waking dreams of memory that so fill our very human days.

The old man was looking beyond himself and I have seen the look before; rarely in the cities where we are too often looking down and in, but often here in the mountains when a man makes eye-contact with the leaping fish, or on a child's face come the first snow, or on mine when the mist floats off the river on a fall morning, or on her's for just a moment a few weeks ago when she looked at me.

THE HOLLOW

The one-room cabin at Lesser Frogpond sits at the edge of a swale, a little thing really, a shallow nest in the aspen and lava over and back of the river, but a pretty thing of itself. Quiet. The bench and slopes of the swale are just enough to swallow any of the distant road noise. In the hardwood mountains back east they call such a place a hollow. And so it is this time of year; a hollow, a place and a sound and a feeling.

Winter came back to Island Park last week fetching over-the-knee new snow and yipping up the last big holiday until spring. They're gone now, the many of them, back down to places that are surely less than this place. It is quiet now and the moon is big and early and full, making an old-time woodcarving of the hollow, the moonlight and shadows sharp and edged and cold. Carved and still. Aspen and pine shadows coming up and across my window. The nights have gone cold again and the old cat has stopped parading the dark and is back before the stove.

An owl has come to the hollow this week. Just one, a big shape in the moonlight, a horned owl, I think, but maybe big enough to be a great grey. Owls court at this time of year, calling across the forest to each other in musical thirds and fifths; but this owl is alone and its song has no music, it is a dry hoot, a solitary's call, after the flying squirrels that live in the cabin walls perhaps. The new snow has smothered all the sound at distance so the hollow lifts the voice of the owl up, swale to cabin to valley walls. It is a magic thing, this quiet moonlight between storms back here, tucked into deep winter with stove and cat. But the owl is a bother. The voice of the owl in the hollow.

The coyotes have been coming in from valley edges. A friend had them outside his cabin last week, many of them, chattering and whooping their way through the snow to what was left of a deer from the autumn hunt. Hungry coyotes under a cold moon. It is an untidy time. Maybe the false promise of spring a few weeks ago got their blood a-rush and stirred things too high for them, and now they are hungry with much winter left.

I think it is more hollow this year because we came so close to a spring melt just two weeks ago. The sun-warmth churned up and the top layers of the snowpack turned to sugar in my hand. The heart of the stuff started to melt from the bottom up, and I almost smelled green late one afternoon and so did the trees and the ground. When the cold came back I'll bet there was a little space, a hollow, a shadow, between the blue-white bottom snow and the wishing ground, that could catch sound like a cupped palm every-where. And so the voice of the owl is magnified again from stirring ground to swale to cabin to valley walls.

It is an untidy time of year, the where and the what of your life cluttered from the close habits of winter quarters. I cannot possibly wish for more than I have, which is now beyond what I ever dared wish for in a long life of wishes. But I do and am shamed by it. The hollow is so much more beautiful when it is filled; filled with aspen leaf and birds and sun all gold with heat, the hollow throwing up to the cabin the pulsing hurry of the river far below. But now there is only silver and white-cold and a bothersome owl croaking out in the dark where the snow is too hollow and too deep to even give back an echo.

An Opera of Swans

It's just plain cooties getting old. Especially in February. Especially with four and a half feet of snow on the level outside. Especially with the woodpile crawling farther away from the cabin and getting furtive and coy during the storms. Especially when I dig out the poor little cache and find that even the wood is old wood: you know, the stuff that is brown and mold-stained on both ends, been laying around on the bottom of things too long so it's frozen harder than a pagan's heart, and is so dense with rot that it weighs more than a guilty conscience.

I was struck down with sloth last autumn when the time came for stacking and am now being visited by that sin of neglect. Lesser Frogpond looked so happy then with stove wood strewn in piles all over the yard. The old cat and I would take in the afternoon on the porch and watch all the merry squirrels and butterflies dashing around in the gaps of the askew woodpiles and it all looked fine and lazy and in the droning sunlight we could think of ten or so things that didn't need doing without even getting ourselves up.

Then winter came often and early and the squirrels went to bed and so did the woodpiles and soon there was nothing but rounded shapes out there under the belt-high snow to give clues about where to dig someday. Someday showed up too soon.

That fall I had peeled the skins on some Ashton onions and chewed local aspen buds and checked the height of the river willows and measured around in the cat's fur and pondered over all the other signs and started splitting wood one day and stacking it neatly on the porch until the cabin began to list a little more than normal toward the swale, but the sun was warm and I could hear the fish calling up in the canyon, so I put the ax aside and picked up the rod and never quite got back to the chores. But I'd forgotten, again, to insulate the hovel as I've been meaning to do for over ten years now, and when the cold came, it came right on in, again. The split and stacked porch wood got gobbled right on up to keep a glow on the little stove, and right after Christmas I had to go out digging in the yard, again.

I have gotten to feeling old without getting to feel important, so I can't blame anyone except myself for the wood that keeps burrowing away in the yard. I've always meant to rotate that old musky stuff up closer to the cabin so I could burn it early before it went to punk, but those fish sing so pretty in the fall under the golden aspen, that I didn't get around to it, again. And now it is cold and all that is left of the once rich hoard of fresh bright-burning wood is the old orphan wood, out at the edges of the property, somewhere. Wood that is just a shade too long, by the way, since I had cut those loads when I was running short on saw-gas and was getting arm-light from wrestling the machine. The fish were singing up in the canyon, so I cheated just a little and cut them some long, and now I've got to fold and cuss and convince them into the stove at challenging angles.

I suppose the ordeal of the old distant wood is healthy and therapeutic: I can frustrate around out in the storms, bloodhounding around for wood that will be all smoke and little heat, and feel that I am doing my bit to save humanity. Especially local humanity: you see, every year at this time, when the wood and I get old, my attitude gets a little tense, and having this winter hobby at home—alone—helps. Life in the mountains is very good for refining one's attitudes: I, for instance, have achieved a state of mental health where suicide is unthinkable but murder, especially in late February, can be attractive; so it's good to play hide-and-seek out in yard to take the edge off of things a little.

There is a bright side, as always, to this adversity. The cat and the stove never seem to remind me about the wood until after sundown. I cuss very quietly, even in four and a half feet of snow, since I might miss the wood snickering at me and it might get away. The swans like to group up at this time of year in the open water at the tail end of the Box Canyon down in Last Chance. This week the moon is waning and late getting up the sky, and they call to each other often out in the cold dark, perhaps to determine position, perhaps just for comfort.

When I have made the evening capture of logs and am carefully finding my trail back to the cabin by starlight, there is an opera of swans surrounding my home, court music for the kingdom, to remind me of who and where I am. An opera of swans as old the mountains and just as grand, that I might not hear and heed as well if I were tucked against the stove with wood ready to hand. Perhaps I won't stack the wood next year either. Again.

PIG-WING BLACKBIRDS

"Four and Twenty Blackbirds Baked in a Pie..."
—from an ancient rhyme

Ten years ago I enjoyed their melodious trilling as a chirp-felt harbringer of spring. This year I've decided they all need a muffler on their exhaust systems and I am considering putting out rat poison to calm down the plague of feathered rodents. They conduct organized dive-bomber raids on the old cat and peck at his porchy naps. They rattle the cabin walls and my comatose composure with their dawn cacophony of honks and shrieks. They eat a hundred pounds of bird seed before noon. They blacken the thin trees at Lesser Frogpond like runt vultures waiting for another bag of gourmet eed to die open. They pester the hand that feeds them. The old truck looks like it has white measles. When the seed runs out they line the windowsill like an Alfred Hitchcock movie. I have chickadees and squirrels hiding in the cabin, soon the moose will be next. They need to get a job. They need to go away.

They're called red-wing blackbirds, though properly there are several varieties. Some have just the deep scarlet bands on both shoulders, others when stretched out (while trying to kill each other or any polite passer-by) show yellow or even white bands next to the red. Their cousins, the yellow-headed blackbirds (they have a cry like a train wreck) are decent enough to arrive later in the season and hang out down in putrid swamps where they belong. Eventually the red-wings join them there and they all fight constantly at loud volume over territory, their woven basket nests deep in the long grass, the birds popping up to complain every few minutes like black fleas in the reed-fur of the still water.

Blackbirds winter far south in the grain-acres of central California and forever rice-fields of Alabama and Mississippi. They wait until they hear me open the last precious bag of black-oil sun-flower seeds for the chickadees and then rush like Huns for my porch. Black Locusts. They must be related by some snide twist of evolution to locusts.

As if the commotion and greed weren't enough, the bull black-birds conduct vulgar courtship right out the window in front of the cat, who is quite prissy about such things. The males suck in the gut, pull up the shoulders, prop out their wing elbows and do a startling imitation of toreadors in the bullring. A friend of the female flavor has remarked that they resemble me in her parlor on Saturday afternoons, but she is underwhelmed with passion for me and knows not what she speaks. The male birds strut around for hours while the females graze quietly on the food I've put out—which also sounds familiar, come to think of it.

About the time the buttercups are shining under the last stub-born snowbanks, the blackbirds will rise like a cloud one morning and be gone, back into the open water deep in the trees where the cat-tails are rising, back far enough to only terrorize deer and grouse and full-grown bears. We'll come out from being cabin-bound by the red-winged blizzard and plant our flag back on the porch and take in the spring mornings with only the sweet lullabye of the early mosquitoes to pleasure us.

Then there are the cowbirds.

SETTLING IN

It is an astonishment that this place, this valley, becomes more dear to me as the years fall by. Well more than ten years now, in all the seasons, and I have not yet grown used to this place, not grown careless with what I see. Each year the roots pull deeper and I find it harder to leave the cherishing for even a day. Perhaps it is that the furniture of the country has been rearranged and tumbled so often during the years of my watch: The Great Fires of 1988, The Great Blizzard of that same winter, the beetle and the dying of the forest, the silent white deep winters of '83 and '84 and the beginning of the new forest. Bears gone thin and bears gone frequent. This is a place that will not abide getting used to, and so I am still just settling in.

And so, when some have asked where I intend to go on my vacation—the second voluntary one in nearly eight years—I am astonished. Why, here, of course. This is my home and there is much yet to do and see. Spring has arrived by the calendar for the first time since I have been here and so there is time, quiet precious time, in this gap between the snow season and the thousands who will come in late May, come because they want to vacation in the same place that I do. I shall go for a walk in the woods.

In all the other years of mine, late March has been a time for the snow to turn to old pudding: too sour to be of much use but not so ripe that winter has been ready to throw it away. This year, with the frost chased off, the snow is not running off as much as it is running in; dripping straight into the ground and waking the wildflowers. There are still yards of snow up high that will linger, as always, into summer, but the lower forest is clearing out and calling everyone home.

I've never felt comfortable leaving the bears alone in their long night, but now they are up and out. The yard is plenty with robins and soon the sandhill cranes will be dancing and jumping back in the meadows, and there can be no finer place or time to be than here in the mountains.

I was driving the long road across the Henrys Lake Flats last Monday and got caught in a cloud of bluebirds. I reached my hat out the window and whooped a shout at speed, the wind folding the bright birds around and safely away from the truck, and felt alive and in joy.

There are tiny frisky springs back on Thurmon Ridge that will only run for a few weeks now, and deer called back by the hundreds after their winter in the desert to the sweet water. The osprey will return and acrobat the April storms. Blue and yellow violets will only bloom for a few days and must be searched out of their hiding places. The hawk that I raised at Lesser Frogpond will sail onto the porch some morning soon to linger for a day or so before moving up the Box Canyon to her summer quarters. So much is waking up from winter—even me.

Besides, she has eyes the color of butterscotch and an intelligence as wild and proud as my mountains, and I want to walk her in the woods. We'll speak to each other long and slowly and settle in.

EASTER BLUSHES

My grandfather, Tom, knew how to call hogs, find water with a peach wand, and mind his own business. I've never tried any of those things so I don't know if they were passed down to me. Tom could also whistle up flowers, and I am puckered out from the trying all week and have cussedly failed. Maybe Tom kept that talent away from the bloodlines or maybe, certainly, he was a better whistle man than I am.

My family used to go back to Oklahoma to visit Tom and his family in the late summer, when school was still out and his crops were filling fine without much tending, the time of fireflies and sweet melons in that country. But one year, when I was about poppin-jay age, we went in the spring, when the red old dirt of that place was just winking awake. I remember hanging onto Tom's hand and walking the evening roads while he pointed out fresh new rabbits in the hedgerows and told me Easter stories and waved a long arm at the wild coloring sky he taught me to love. One of our first walks that spring I made a child's greedy complaint about how the greened-up borrow ditches beside the road didn't have any of the flowers he had shown me in my grandmother's seed catalog the night before. Tom pulled himself all the way down to me and said they were damsels, these wildflowers, and they must be coaxed a little, courted he said.

So Tom and I sat in the noon on the edge of the ditch by the road and he whistled and kept time with his hand on the side of his knee. It was an old Ozark tune called Cripple Creek, and I can still play it on the banjo.

The next morning early I snuck out alone to the ditch and there were flowers. Little yellow and blue ones. It was the kind of accident from which real magic is made, and I have never forgotten it. Later in the day on our walk, Tom made me look up and down the road to make sure it was empty, and we gathered a hat-full of those flowers. Stolen flowers are best, Tom said, just a little bit risky and naughty and my grandmother liked things like that, Tom said, and someday someone would like them from me too and we took them home and she did. I didn't mention that he'd whistled them up the night before and neither did he; Tom was not a bragging man, but I have never forgotten.

The neighbor's flowers are being obstinate. Stubborn and sullen and full-of-refusal flowers. I have whistled banjo tunes until the stones danced, I have whistled Beethoven and Brahms, whistled show tunes in five-part harmony, whistled lonesome ballads until the river wept, but the neighbor's tulips won't bloom.

An early spring in Island Park is a puzzle to all who live and would grow here. Many things set their clocks to the angle and duration of sunlight—the aspen are just starting, for instance—and don't worry over the peculiarities of our mountain weather for their comings and goings. But tulips are flashy dancers and will bloom up the town given opportunity. Tulips in Island Park are just a bit risky and naughty and will come out when others stay home. This patch is a crimson variety, as red as a first fast love, and our warm spell had the whole green of the plants up and coming—everything but the stealing parts—when a little cold snap hit last week and they dug in their roots and now they won't budge. An old saint-person once said the reward of patience is patience, but I think that's a bunch of hooey in this case, because I've got big plans for those damn tulips.

I started the tradition a few years ago when the cat and I were breathing more smoke than heat from one of those iffy spring fires in the woodstove down at Lesser Frogpond. I looked down at the cat and said: the kingdom is chock-full of damsels. He agreed, having damseled around some in his kittenish youth down in Pinehaven. I said: it has been too white too long and they are all fine females and something should be done right away. The cat, who is frightened by labor, ignored me and went outside where it was chilly, but cleaner and quieter.

I put on my go-raiding hat and went forth. Daffodils and tulips are best and have some weight to the hand and staying power when femaled off. There are some good gardens in this town with cheery yellow and red crops just asking to be bundled up and shared. (Yes, I asked permission, but you've still got to sneak them away to get it done right.) And then it was off in the old truck and up and down the road handing out flowers from the window. Some of the damsels looked almost distressed since I didn't know some of them and I look a little rustic and tangled to be brandishing posies, but I wasn't the point and the flowers grew fine smiles. Some of the ladies were married, some of them pretty and some of them handsome, some them wearing their years well, but Tom was right, because presented with stolen flowers, they all blushed young.

Now if the tulips would just bloom.

We have met the enemy...

A curl-headed sprite lingered the other day to ask me why a robin had been crashing itself into one of her cabin windows up by Macks Inn and why, shoo as she might and often, the poor bird returned in just a few minutes to keep bashing away. I said that she would have to hang something over the window—probably on the outside—for a few days until the bird compulsed elsewhere. I said almost all birds mate at this time of year and her pest was almost certainly a male who was defending his chosen nesting territory from other robins, just like the ones you can see playing judo with each other in the afternoon out in the yard. But in this case, the bull robin was defending against an enemy that was his own reflection, his own image. I suggested that before she cloak her window, she might want to bring by any of her male friends to see if they could apprehend anything meaningful by watching the fool bird.

A little background: the mis-named American robin is really a thrush, young robins for instance have the typical breast-spotting, like a fawn deer, of the thrush family. The thrush family is not long on brains as birds go (raptors, owls and woodpeckers win top honors); and robins operate mostly on what we used to call 'instinct', meaning their behaviour is programmed, and their responses, especially during the critical breeding season, are hard-wired. The robin finds an area that has enough of the right stuff, something in the wiring defines the size of the territory, and other robins become a priority problem. Since the robin in the window doesn't run off or affect a submissive posture, he keeps getting attacked over and over again, even at great price.

Two other species of bird are also famous for having window compulsions, they don't live here but have magnificent names: brown towhees and pied wagtails. Like the robins, thay have a conspicuous eye ring that can be seen even on surfaces of low reflection. That may be why I've never been able to stop the robin-bashing by hanging a towel or drawing the curtains; there is still enough reflection for the bird to see the white eye-ring and key the response, so I've always had to go outside and block off the window itself.

Robin's aren't just bull-stubborn about windows, there are some peculiar stories about their nesting habits. One famous (and photo-documented) tale is about the robin who nested on the arm of an oil-rig in Michigan. The bird probably built the nest when the arm was at rest but when the eggs were laid the the programming took over and, when someone finally noticed, it had hatched and was rearing young on a working arm that moved up and down nine feet every few minutes. A family in Colorado had to remove the side-view mirror of their old Ford in the driveway and mount the thing on a post because a robin kept insisting on building a nest in the crook of the mirror and they needed to use the car. The bird raised a family happily on the post by the driveway while the car went on chores. In just a week or so, Tony Scarpelli in Last Chance will have to park his junker work-truck for a spell because every year a robin demands to nest in one of the wheel-wells. They are a stubborn lot, these robins, sometimes even a trifle stupid.

There is an educational irony here, of course. The female bird will nest how and when she pleases and achieve a singularity of egg-mind even in adversity. The male will rooster up for battle and get pushy about his rights and possessings even when he is fighting his own self-image and so become his own worst enemy. I have done so myself too often. It is another lesson of the mountains that you pay a price for not paying attention and adjusting. Most of the time the robins get the job done, but there are certainly more happy ways to do it. Like the birds, I can never win fighting myself, but I can surely lose. It is a foolhardy contest, all posture and no substance.

So I told the young honey-eyed lady to bring her friends by that they might see themselves in the bird in her window. I have.

RENAISSANCE IN MAY

Island Park is going through a renaissance this week. A rebirth. Again. It is these seasons that are my ground-wire, my touchstone and timepiece. And these changings of the seasons in Island Park are always different, each of its own, different, and so the turnings are my guide, the changes changing me.

You know how it is when you enter a room you have long known, a deeply familiar place, where you immediately notice anything moved or changed or different. I have a place like that here in Island Park and this week things, even the light, are being moved and changed there.

In the few miles between my home and the newspaper office there is an old road, part of what people call the Old Highway, that I drive and walk in the un-snow times, or snowshoe and ski in the winter. Of the few who drive it, very few slow down on the old road; it is a dirty old road, washboarded and cracked with some gravel here and there to keep you attentive on steering. Most of it runs through clear-cut log sales of twenty or thirty years past and does not concern the eye. The river runs nearby but is always out of sight. Now in May, there are a few mud-puddle ponds and a pair of skitterish mallard ducks. Come September there will be dry-hot acres of grasshoppers and dust. To most, it is just an old road in the brush.

But I have grown fond of the old road, keen on it, familiar with its moods and little ways. A few hundred feet from the road there is a startling few feet of sudden douglas fir and chipmunks and the cliff, and then down and away and noisy, the Box Canyon of the river. A fisherman-moose-pilgrim footpath runs along the top of the cliff in the fir shadows and I have a small fire ring on a lava heave that sits across from a plain-simple waterfall on the other bank of the river. It is a thoughtful place where I have watched generations of red squirrels, flying squirrels by evening, grey jays and chickadees in the winter, and from a clump of scragg aspen no larger than my cabin, seen new white-tail deer emerge each year.

When I walk the cliff trail it is like you walking into the familiar room, something moves a little or is a little different and you notice. I notice there are more fish this year. This year they rise at any hour, a happiness of fish after the bugs and moths of a hot, early spring. The ground squirrels, gophers some call them, seem to have peaked in their cycle this year and they are everywhere and underfoot, chirping to each other, drawing a sky-full of hawks the way the moths have called the fish. One of the hawks I raised years ago came from a dying aspen by the old road.

One morning this week I drove the old road, slowly, and was comfortable with it; a new burrow, badger maybe, has emerged out in an east meadow, I saw it just as I would see a book moved from one of my bookshelves. The mule deer are back from the desert and I stopped to pull back some old fireweed to see the tracks where I knew they would cross the old road. A few buttercups hid in the old stalks held over under the snow from last summer. A hawk watched me pass, maybe one of those I had known. The meadows looked ready.

That afternoon, coming home, I stopped just after starting down the old road, and gawked. In just a few hours, the meadow had come into a renaissance: satin-purple shooting stars and butter-yellow glacier lillies and violets, by hell, more violets than I had ever seen in any year before. I ditched the truck and walked out into the waste of old stumps and slash piles as filled as a Christmas morning.

They are never the same, these springs in the mountains. And how did the old road know that violets are my darlings dear: violets and country gardens, violets and fairy tales, violets and butterflies and books and small water creeks. I lay down under a tree and a hawk. Violets and hermits, violets and love, on an old road deep in the mountains.

HALFWAY HOME

O n the date of this issue of this newspaper, I shall have come forty-five years old. It is not one of those mileposts you ignore easily—or safely. I had the honor of editing an Island Park newspaper when I turned forty and I wrote some piece of fluff then, no doubt infested with bravado wit and whimsy, that I cannot find, thank God, for it would not do for a model. There is weight in forty-five, the end of the rope on young-fool excuses and growing up. Leaf and twig, for better or worse, you are grown at forty-five. As with the rest of us, there have been prices exacted for being allowed to remain alive this long, but especially these last few years, especially in this place, the rewards—many undeserved and unasked for—have been well worth all the costs down all the years. I have chosen my ancestors carefully, a folk with sturdy genetics, and can expect, barring accident and idiocy, to live into my ninetys. Halfway home. I have nested my heart in the mountains, am very happy, and am only halfway home.

It has been, and is, a fitful and enduring pilgrimage. Because of in-born stubborness and stunting pride, some of the leaves opened late and I began my adult years here in Island Park. I am having such a fine time, thank you, that I hope to end them here also. There have been mornings when these mountains were the top of the world, some where this place seemed the edge of the world, and a very few that I was sure heralded the end of the world, but this is where I live, by choice and devotion. I have found something that I did not know I was looking for but now know I need: A life in a place like this and the place of mind it creates. I am looking out the window of the cabin at Lesser Frogpond at snow falling, in insistent quantity, on the buttercups and violets and summer birds outside. It is endearing, this place.

But enough of that; at this last gasp of adolescence I have something to report:

Take heart. We all really do understand each other.

I have been writing these little ditties for nearly ten years now. Our mountains are large enough to contain a treasure of subject matter, including what we might be for and to each other. It might seem peculiar to write about human relationships in wild mountain metaphors, but there is much that is yet wild and free-flying in all of us, and the largeness of this valley overcomes knee-jerk opinions, so it has seemed a safe place for us to chat.

I've written in the first person because I cannot presume to speak for you, the editorial 'we' is a sterile burden, and I do not socialize enough for team pronouncements. I've sometimes run the edge on this corner of the page because I can afford the emotional risk: the cat is constant and I have been long convinced of my own foolishness. Being this close to the sky can open feelings and make them plain. I have written about things I needed to know, like wondering whether the path to another's heart ran through our forests and winter stars. There have been columns that sent me to the dictionary and out to the porch for a head-scratch, and I apologize for having been often difficult, and apologize even more for still not having the answers to the questions, but something wonderful and un-looked for has happened out of it all.

Especially these last years, your newspaper receives a lot of mail. A surprising amount of it is personal, well, sort of personal. Most is from people I have never met who (they say) enjoy the newspaper, and will write a short note, or scribble the back of a card, and say things that defy distance. A woman in Connecticut once wrote to tell me about a death in World War I in France and how something in a column had made her feel less alone. I have never been in Europe or in her sad war, I am nothing special, a hermit-sometimes-scholar pecking away in the trees, a role thousands of years old and not unusual. Yet this woman and I felt special about something difficult, and special in the same way enough that we understood each other. After her letter, I did not feel so alone either.

A small girl and her mother were in my office this week. I have let my hair grow long for reasons I do not quite understand. (Having written that, I see it is a lie: while I was going to seed this spring, a lady looked at me working in my half-glasses and noted a certain resemblance to 17th century Ben Franklin—complete with bald spot—and it touched my vanity—a thing of some push in a man my age—and there is the truth.) The little girl took her head to one side, like they do, and peered at me; hair and half-glasses and worn cloth shirt. I set her in the old oak office chair and gave her the plastic moose that guards the telephone. "I'll bet you think I look like a silly old fool," I said. She looked down at the moose and nodded. "It's all right, my dear," I said, "I really am a silly old fool." She looked up and smiled and we laughed and so we understood each other.

A very regal lady, proud with years, walked in the office one day and, after our business was done, quietly told me how she had clipped a column and put it on her bedstand all one painful February in her home on the west coast. I do not know which one it was, it would have been graceless to ask and she did not offer, but the shared understanding was enough.

I have pondered over the thing: there can be an intimacy between writers and readers. It is a one-on-one sharedness, the pages read alone, just as they are written alone. There is no need for the pretenses of physical presentaion; the lacey screen of ink let's us tell each other secrets. And we humans can have so much common understanding: love wrapped in aspen leaf and called pretty as a mountain moon is not so different from aged hands holding in a grey farmhouse on the plains of Kansas. I have been told so, and believed and understood them, and it often has taken me from despair to delight. The pain of separation or loss is the same whether standing on the dark seashore or huddled in a blizzard-wrapped cabin. We can understand each other very well, if we choose to share our secret dreams and fears. And joys.

These are changing times. In the mountains and other places of people, it may become difficult and frightening. I am happy to report, come halfway home, that we are not alone.

WAGONS FULL OF WISHES

I read this week where scientists have found ardent proof of a black hole at the center of a distant galaxy. They cannot see the thing of course; black holes are so dense and compelling that even light cannot escape their gravity, but they can see in this one galaxy, for the first time, where things are becoming brightly Not; stars and wheels of blazing matter turning and falling into dark pit half the size of our solar system, a hungry ghost of a thing eating everything in its corner of the universe. It is only 30 million light years away, this thing of nothing that pulls away anything, and I have decided that this black hole is no doubt the cause of our peculiar weather, that it has somehow pulled at the fulcrum of wind that lives in the south of our valley and has changed things that we once thought we knew.

I admire these late September days in Island Park. I would admire them more if it was not early July. On the first of this month some of the fireweed began to bloom around the porch at Lesser Frogpond. I went out and tried to shoo the flowers off, into August where they belong for instance, but they insisted, and there are more every morning. Just today, word has come of huckleberries ripening out in the forest, and we all know that it is a fool huckleberry that will bare itself to early summer, but they have come. The sego lillies are early also, early and many. Even old-timers are out searching the woods, one hand to their brow, their circadian clocks dashed against the untimeliness of things, a confusion of colors telling lies on the season.

We are justly, if vainly, proud of being different in Island Park; it is mostly our forest only that has this damp fever, ours within these high valley walls. The lower valley has been spit at by a few clouds and moved around some by winds in a hurry, but those two pil-grims were coming here to spend time with us: Island Park has received over six inches of rain in the last four weeks while sur-rounding areas have just been skipped. Much that was asleep these last years of drought has come awake.

The early bloomings and berries have, of course, led to dire mutterings of doom in the taverns and around the nail bins in the lumber yards. All the signs and omens point to a heavy winter beginning next Wednesday. I grew thoughtful and went out for an evening stroll in the Box Canyon to check for bugling elk (heard none, but saw a snowshoe hare that looked suspiciously poised to molt into white). The local woodcutters are doing a brisk business and woodpiles are beginning to appear in July yards as the flowers-that-won't-shoo drive men to desperate hoarding. The cat and I walked the grounds this afternoon counting cords; down at Lesser Frogpond we like to store our wood standing straight up and there are five or six cords of fine dead dry lodgepole that hasn't fallen over yet, with winter kindling even provided by the dry cones at the end of their branches. It seems to us that is somehow more effi-cient, and less tiring, to store emergency winter wood that way.

All this anxiety is low-oxygen mountain nonsense though. The black hole that has twisted the wind has no doubt demented us also, because there is a plain answer for all these forest mysteries and I think it is this: we have all been in love and can remember that it is a heady feeling indeed. I have been in love—the truth be told I still am—but I have been in touching/seeing/handholding love and it accelerated and enhanced everything about me and the time. When I was bereft of her it was a dry and hollow plodding of days. We, all of us—leaf and claw and man, have seen several dry years in a row and that lack had stretched us. But now the rain has come and, like the love that is a nourishing fuel, the water has hurried us, made the berries dizzy with joy, called out the flowers at their best, and made the forest bold. Love will make of life plenty, and the clouds have come like wagons filled with wishes, and made hasty blossoms of us all.

By the way, it will be a long full summer. The eaves and corner notches of Lesser Frogpond are filled with wrens, my favorite little birds of summer, wise and graced with music. The first crop of young wrens is out tumbling around the yard teasing the old cat, and the adults are starting on new clutches of eggs for a second go at wrenning-up the world. They never do that when a winter will come early, so I will shoo no more flowers this year.

EPIPHANY

Early last year a friend started to lose the edges around his seeing and he went to some people and they told him that he might lose a lot of his sight, maybe even he could lose it all. Eventually, it turned out they were wrong, but he told me some things that seemed peculiar—too simple—until I found my own context out in the trees the other day, in a place long familiar, where I found something growing that—like his sight—I thought I might have lost.

They gave him some glasses that brought things back for a while and he said they were wonderful and that once he was done feeling sorry for himself, he became greedy for the looking of things, and he went out and saw things, looked hard at things until the old became new. He said he was afraid that there was too much that he might not see again, but rather than gorge on new places and scenery, he wanted to see the familiar things and places, wanted to take the time to see them whole, instead of rushing by as if they would be there forever.

He said all this busy new looking started to change him one day: Instead of using the things around him carelessly, he was forced to pay attention so well that he ended up serving those things with his looking. Maybe, he said, that is why his vision eventually never left him. It did not need to since it was no longer his, he said.

My first years here in the mountains were times of plenty. We had a treasure of snow those years and fish rolled heavy in the river and the elk sang all night long in the fall and I played with the bears in summer. I suppose I was aware that they were fat years; I would hear the old-timers talk about the storms being frequent and wild, hear them brag on the many feet of snowpack, hear pilgrim fisherman glow with fish stories that were even true. But I had no context for those years; I was proud to be here and proud to begin collections of my own fine stories, proud to make history between me and this place. But I did not know.

Then came the beetle and the drought and the fires and more drought and winters too thin to hold stories. I remembered the good years but I could not remember them enough, because I had not been looking well. I thought then that this place would always be so full, and so I used the forest hastily, because it would always be there.

Nearly eight inches of moisture has come to Island Park in the last eight weeks. In winter that would be eight to ten feet of snow. It is a feast. Last week I found a flower in the deep forest and suddenly remembered the good years. It was a monkshood, a flower so poisonous that even handling it brusquely brings some risk. Monkshood is as tall as my throat and bears flowers the color of old blood and topaz. In this area there is no other color in nature like it, a purple so deep it looks lethal, and a man who is looking can see it from far off, even years far off. I went and held the blossoms lightly and toed the soil: like many poisonous things, monkshood favors the dark wet places. Purple against the new green of the new pine forest, aspen whispering green shadows, the tracks of deer in the moist dirt. I have not seen monkshood since the good years, and seeing it helped me recall them and know, now, that this was a good year also for my home. The friend had said it was too simple, and now I saw it, so I looked longer and quietly and welcomed the flower home. For just a lingering moment, I was the servant of a poisonous flower in the green growing woods.

After the forest I went and found her and she looked well. There is willow in her, I thought, willow in her shape and movings. I suppose I had noticed it before, but never enjoyed it so much, the familar bendings of an arm of her seen new. She is not graceful, she is more: coltish and eager in her ways, and she comes to my throat and is as sweet of her own color, now seen, as my dark flower in the trees.

QUICKSILVER AND GOLD

A small wind came down from the aspened lava bench behind Lesser Frogpond last week and pooled clean air in the long grass at the base of the cabin. The old cat and I went out under the moon with naked feet and padded about in the cool of it, the slow puddles of breeze not yet light as frost, but sweet and fresh to the touch after these last hot nights. The cat pounced after moths and mice in the foxtail weeds and I lay down with the yarrow and clover adoring the light and the time. There is no place like home, sang the woman on the radio when I was a child. There is no place like home, said the man to his moon this night.

The moon followed a yellow star and the dew followed the wind and the cat followed me as we went inside after he had pressed up to me and I had nodded and gathered an arm-load of wood from the edges of the yard. There were small signs of autumn and we built a small fire in the stove, comforted by the light and simple ritual. Moonlight and firelight and the cat on the knee.

It rained without thunder last week, rained slow and quietly, and drew the hurried violence out of summer. The next day I lay in the heat by water, pushed down dormant by the noon of the summer and the hot steel shine off the river. I rolled over and out to the northwest noticed high clouds the color of quicksilver. It is now many years since this valley claimed me and if you have invested your heart in a person or place the love will help you notice more carefully, listen and watch more keenly, as the years come ripe. It is love that makes the difference between the familiar and the cherished. I noticed these clouds coming home because it is the color of quicksilver in their folds that first announces autumn, and I cherish that time in this place.

So much magic now: I heard a tweet last evening across the river in the Box Canyon and I had to lean against a doug fir to save energy for my grinning. The little elk have started, the cub scouts of their tribe, trying young voices that crack with uncertainty and eagerness out in the meadows of Harriman Park while the old bulls lay high up under the aspen and patiently wait for the time. The little elk squeel and tweet and the sound is endearing in its fervent sincerity, but when the nights come shiver-cold and the moon is high, the bulls will come down to the meadows and begin the old old music of high notes that raise your hair and drum-grunts you feel in your belly. I wonder about their peculiar lust of autumn, a thing of no choices or confusion, an unwavering blood-driven combat and pairing as certain as the stars. There is much power in that certainty, a security of shared cadence of pulse, but the song is not soft and the time not cherishing. For old elk and young poets, autumn is a rush of self-destruction, a sacrifice of the self to passion. I listen to them often at night and wonder over how simple their rituals must be.

She has hair the color of aspen gone golden and a mind as fine and exquisite as quicksilver. Can you promise forever without conflict or compromise, she sang. No, I said, and the elk cried in the dark. I can promise you will be cherished forever, just as this moon adores your cheek, but I cannot promise that which you ask. She smiled and there were small signs of autumn in my heart. I can promise that you are so rare that unicorns will forever come to lay their heads in your lap, I said to the dark where she had been.

It is better to love a place, I said to the elk across the river and under the trees, and went home and built a small fire and placed the cat on my knee.

She Did Not Smile So Well

The year started coming ripe last week in our mountains. A hard frost slipped into the valley, following the stars, Pleiades rising. It was fourteen degrees in Shotgun Valley, less than twenty at Lesser Frogpond, under thirty on the banks of Henrys Lake. The small kitchen gardens lay down and the bugs whispered in their nests deep in long grass.

The aspen is our harlequin, our painted lady, our jester mocking the young idea of summers that never end. The aspen leaf is tropistic—born and dying of the light—but its mood is ruled by air; the frost comes and pinches each one in passing, leaving a bruise, a last golden blush where touched, before the leaf falls away. The frost last week was uneven magic, changing some and forsaking others. Cold air flows like silent water, flows down and fills the low places, the difference of a few feet in height sparing more summer for berry and leaf. There is a small strong aspen in the swale below my cabin that went golden the morning after the cold, while the trees above remained a fine raving green. The cat and I padded through the silver-frosted weeds to cheer the tree's passing and we sat on the chill rocks, my hand against the cat's muzzle which has silvered this year, so like my own beard, so like the morning. We were a fine fall canvas, the silver and the little golden tree, harlequins all, each a color of the mountains.

It is these mornings that make me sad for the year come ripe in lesser places. The cities come to autumn almost unknowingly, since there is poor taste in their changing color that is only a patina of stain. But even the great grain fields below us and the tended miles of hay are all of one color, come of one time. The fields are magnificently golden but all of one piece and too subtle.

The plains are plain, but the patchworked patterns of the year come ripe in the mountains seem so like the seasons of a man: this tree green, this one gold; the knees and face touched with frost, the heart and mind—if grace and humor allow—grown well ripe and full.

Real beauty is complex, a happy meeting of imperfections and rogue details. Our mountains have that high beauty because the frost is choosy and coy in this place of slopes, so we are rich in silver and green and gold. The trees here live at the edge, where security and sameness are thin, and only these extremes of place can offer such extremes of beauty.

If she did not smile so well, I would be gone out among the trees at this season, following the trail of frost, tracking the times I love. Some trees and I share the intimacy of secrets. There is an aspen in the Box Canyon that I visit at this time and admire the one side gone gold. I slept beneath that tree one night and the frost found me, just as it found the tree's one side, flowing down a small rise in the sagebrush before turning away. It is a secret, a knowing intimacy that the tree and I share. Or another, which will stay green long into fall because it shares the river's warm breath from below, just as I have in that spot under a cold moon. An intimacy, a knowing.

But she smiles so well in the cabin's one chair that I can often only wonder after my trees and their colors, caught in this season of her smile. She smiles as if we shared a secret though I cannot imagine what it could be. I do not remember ever being where she is, for I am so silver and she is so fair. I cannot track her heart, so I get up and put another log in the stove, hoping the frost will never touch her and she will, for warmth alone, never go away.

Empty Nests and Conepiles

We have arrived at the finest confluence of our mountain seasons: the early chill bite of late September folding into full fall. The Milky Way is turning like a great wheel, bending to an east-west axis, the shining starpath coming brightest of the year early next month. When we look at the Milky Way we are looking from edge to heart of our home galaxy; we out far on a spiraling arm looking into a bright discus of busy burning stars. I spend much time out looking into the night and there is a pleasing vertigo—like being in a carnival car that rotates against the horizon—to watching the arc of the galaxy wheel slowly to the tune of the seasons.

There is such an astonishment of aspens this year; they loved the gift of a summer's water and have returned us the pleasure of autumn's gold. Walking in the Box Canyon in the evenings, when the light is lowing and lush, even the shadows seem to have color, rich purples, satin under the Doug firs, heart-yellow leaves scattered like coins in the grass. The osprey nests across the river have emptied out, the birds have broken from the mountains and, like kites, snapped free to the wind and turned away south. They have departed early, though not alarmingly so: it was a summer of plenty and the young grew well and rapidly and were ready while the winds were still warm.

Last week, while sneaking through the aspen looking for wild scullcap and mint, I stumbled across a magnificent cache of pinecones and dried mushrooms. There were perhaps thirty bushels of booty tucked carefully under and along the big trunk of a fir deadfall, squirrels screeching and scolding over my head and out of the weeds. I ran my hand through the treasure and grinned down the beasts. Squirrels cache on the north side of logs for the same reason bears den up on north-facing slopes: the storage will survive any pesky mid-winter thaw and keep the storage—bear and cone—safe and fresh in their sleep. These harvesters had done well for the pines loved the summer's moisture also and grew plump secret seeds hiding under the bark of the cones. Conepiles in the mountains are, for me, our version of grain bundles shocked in the fields, our pumpkin patches, the picture of autumn set to the music of squirrels and crows.

Another harbinger of autumn appeared last week with the annual publishing of the *Old Farmer's Almanac*, this its 201st edition. As the warden of a previous Island Park newspaper I had the audacity and joy of producing an Island Park almanac for 1988 and take great pleasure in the reading and making of the things. When Ben Franklin brought out the first issue of his Poor Richard's Almanack in 1732, he was in competition with several dozen other regional almanacs for the attention and shilling of a populace that lived much in the outdoors and needed to know things about the larger rhythms of outside. There were not many clocks then (or even accurate calendars) and all the almanacs provided the times of the risings and settings of planets and stars and the moon's phases so that the people of the outdoors could set their affairs in order by cosmic agreement.

Some of us in the mountains accept and enjoy this same sense of timing, and it is a fortunate way to live, I think. We are so far north up the planet here that the bending of the sunlight to our edge of the world is varying and insecure, the length of daylight or closing of night so rapidly changing that a clock on the mantle is more ornament than instrument. I like the almanacs and their tables and schedules of seasons and stars. I can study the small pamphlet by an evening fire and go out and tell the time by the position of the Big Dipper swinging around the north star or the position of bright falling Venus or the rising of a crescent moon. It makes me feel the galaxy a home.

All almanacs try to forecast the coming year's weather (Mr. Franklin's predictions were notoriously inaccurate, which amused him greatly). The *Old Farmer's Almanac* has achieved a reputation (at least) for accurate forecasting—they called the arrival of Hurricane Andrew a year ahead of time, for instance. The coming winter for our region is predicted to be colder than normal with much-above normal snowfall. That would be a poleasure indeed. There were some winters like that in the early 1980's here in Island Park and they were a joy—if you were prepared and your cache was on the north side of things, you were under the cold and the snow most of the time, and we all slept safe and secure.

ON THE FRONTIER

I don't travel much anymore. Oh, I don't mean the trips out into the trees stuff; those kinds of travel are just strolls out in the yard and these last years anywhere inside the volcano walls seems like home, off the porch or outside the cabin window. And Yellowstone is just down the block, a familiar and slightly off-beat part of the neighborhood. Even the two-hundred mile round-trip to Shelley, Idaho, to print your newspaper, has become a smaller pilgrimage; a little jaunty in the winter, but still known territory, a well-worn path.

But I don't journey like I once did; there were many years in other places, time spent on big rivers or across the world, over the seas. I suppose I was caught somewhere between quest and adventure: looking things over, looking for things too, but carried always by the taste of risk, riding exotic. A best friend of the female persuasion in those years cackled once that I was a poor man's cross between Indiana Jones and Pan: a respectable enough rake, but always dashing off to some far somewhere to translate something and try to pipe sloe-eyed dryads out of the foreign trees. And travel in other directions and contexts: universities and rice-fields, sitting at fine tables with too many forks and squatting with the tribes over broiled bugs. Folks like that, folks like me then, always have a certain uneasiness about place, about investing in something or someone for too long. It's not just the thrill of the different—it's also the fear of things becoming the same. Wanderlust is a lust, a passion, another thing driven. But I don't travel much anymore.

And so it is with a small perplexment that I watch so many at this time of year—birds and men and deer—launch off the mountain and sail away. Some leave with excitement and some from good sense, but they all leave—and I just don't see the sense in leaving anymore. I suppose that those with wanderlust or those who veer off the social ladder into lone wolfness are avoiding the horror of being tamed, but now that seems to me a very young thing to think. I spent some good years out on the frontier avoiding a core part of my personality: an embarrassingly gooshy sentimentality that can put me dew-eyed at the sight of violets and young robins. Perhaps I thought it was unmanly or contrary to rugged independence to become too attached to things that the heart goes soft over. I could be fierce in those years and cared deeply and often about ideals and the rightness of things, but none of it was very personal.

Now it is personal. I cannot leave this place because I would too deeply miss the wind in the wild. This place, this last best place, has not tamed those who have come home to here. Each season is a frontier here and it pushes my horizons and pulls the borders out of me to live here. As wild and impossible as these mountains are, they are dear to me and I cling to them and will not be parted.

The poets gush over springtime but I think autumn fetches a deeper passion out on the frontier; even the colors are a ripe joy instead of the flirty hues of April. October is the month where sentiment and passion are well-met, where the known has had time to become beloved, where the things you need are known—wood near the door and elk in the meadow and a cat by the fire and deeply held friendship.

I built a friendship and a passion with the place, and then with her, and discovered that there is a freedom in sentiment, in honest-plain yearning, in never wanting to leave from that place where the heart lives. Last week I stood on an edge of the valley and watched a doe mule deer on the migration trail below. She paused and hesitated often on her way away. Finally she stopped completely, looked out over the mist-washed plains of the lower places, and turned her head up and over her shoulder to look back up to the far ridge I stood on. I turned away then, because I understood the choices of leavings, but her choice was too personal and not mine, so I left without knowing and went back up to home.

LUNACY

The full Hunter's Moon struck last Sunday night. This moon's name—like the Harvest Moon last month—comes from the angle and seeming duration of moonlight; the moon seems higher and brighter and swollen with fullness over three to four nights, thereby letting one harvest or hunt by the longer, bolder light.

Perhaps the light is a little too bright; for thousands of years legends from nearly all cultures have whispered up the full moon as a twisted rudder of human emotions. The Latin word Luna (moon) begat luna-tic and there are some fine old woodcut engravings from the Dark Ages that show a fey beam from the skulking full moon striking the foreheads of pilgrims caught on the road at night, driving them to lunacy. A mischievious physician once noted that we humans are eighty percent water, and water has well-known and predictable tides, and the tidal effect on something made of mostly water will be especially strong at the full moon. So there you are, he said. We're lunatics for sure, he said.

And so it was last Sunday night. The cabin at Lesser Frogpond is positioned to see the ecliptic—path of the moon and planets—out either of the windows. While searching for a book, I took a twirl around the single room that captured the views from both horizons and was beamed over the edge. I went out and called forth my companion from her hermitage and stood out in a field gabbering and pointing in two directions at once. A lunatic in full flower. She, who knows me well, took it all calmly and looked out and over things.

In the west the sun was just leaving us and the harvests in the valley below had gifted the wind with fairy dust and gold, the light was glowing and warm like an evening fire against the hearth of the mountains. In the east the full moon was just rising through the thinnest of gossamer clouds, cold silver, washing the fields with coming frost, regal and rising, pushing the fire in the west over and beyond the edge. I could not see them both without turning so I turned, and turned again, the old cat chasing my feet, pointing at the beautiful lights we live so high up close to. She nodded and laughed, a thing of many bells, and took my hand to still me. She nodded again; yes, she saw. Yes, she knew. The first and the last lights tangled in her hair, silver and gold, and even the cat stopped to look upon her.

I cannot understand why some of these moments of these mountains have not slain me, have not filled me to bursting with too much to bear. The pilgrimage of years has been like Saul's road to Damascus: the beauties of the place striking me down and dumb so often—and yet, it is something I have not grown used to, this raging joy that can come from being here. The rising moon can still set off this kindled rapture, or a ballet of wind in a high pass, or a cherished flight of birds, or the growing light in her eyes.

Monday night the fields were being burned in the valley below and the moon—still full—lifted out of the east on a carriage of smoke, slim runners of yellow-green skating up into the dark. This time she came for me and we went out into the meadow under the slow shadows of the aspen. I think it is not the moon, or the sly pulling of personal water, or even that there is a live volcano beneath my feet, that causes this awed-ful lunacy in me. I think it is the common magic of this place and the filled time. I think it is this simple life that pulls such calmned joy. I think it is the mountains and the touch of the moon in her hair that fills so completely. I think it is a fine and full home.

DRAGONS AND TIGERS AND CHICKADEES

It was an extra-ordinary display of the mountains this last week. The sun is rolling lower along the horizon each day now and the light is pushed to sharp angles, making the shadows steeper, the mountains higher, and the valleys more inclined. The frost on the ground in the mornings was pulled from the cold drying air that night, and dawn blooms all the distant ranges much closer, the Tetons hovering in the chill and Targhee Peak not as far north as usual. It is all ordinary of our autumns and very special.

Coincidental to this time of the year, when our mountains come taller and closer and the rivers can be heard falling down the valleys, last week I stumbled (literally) over a box of books tucked long and dustily away in a corner at Lesser Frogpond. In the box there were books and devices for taking the pulse of the mountains and rivers. I had not taken an extended look at the things in over twenty years, though at one time I made a serious study of (and a few dollars in the practice of) the arcane science of Feng Shui.

Feng Shui (pronounced Fung Shway) is the Chinese system of Geomancy. The words simply mean Wind (Feng) and Water (Shui). It is a very old system of belief: before Confucius there was Feng Shui, before even the porcelain and clay army that was buried with the emperors 4000 years ago there was Feng Shui. It is an ancient theory holding that the fortunes of a cabin or factory or grave or campsite are governed by the lay of the land surrounding, and especially facing, it. The time of the year and position of the stars at the beginning of building (or digging) the project also influence the 'Feng Shui' of the site. Hence, almost all initial plans for construction in China, even to this day, are attended initially by a Feng Shui Man, who will take the pulse and breath of the sky and the land to insure that the currents of good fortune will flow to that direction and place. Much of it seems amusing and arbitrary to western taste, but so did acupuncture (based on a kindred theory of the body) until recent years. I was once, briefly, a Feng Shui Man, and it seems to me there is much sense to much of it.

There is much voodoo and jingle-jangle to the thing, of course, because it is old and wonderful with ritual—and the Feng Shui Man needs to impress the rubes to make his dollar. Most westerners are immediately put off by all the animal symbolism and confusion of color-codes: it is the most excellent Feng Shui, for instance, to build a cabin with the Azure-Blue Dragon on your left and the White Tiger on your right. It is full-bore hideous Feng Shui to have your outhouse door facing, in a straight unbroken line, your cabin front door (thereby attracting purple salamanders, which is very bad indeed). It is permissable, but risky and poor manners, to build anything higher than the surrounding features (making you noticeable to the Black Tortoise, who would be an unfortunate neighbor and would surely freeze your pipes).

What we perceive as a gaudy, overblown imagery is an unfortunate (for us) illusion of the Chinese language, which is rich and plastic in meaning. The characters for 'Black Tortoise', for instance, also signify a time of the year (winter), a direction (north), a thermal affinity (very cold), and a place (low slope). To the initiate, the whole confusing thing is a kind of computational shorthand: trigonometry with dragons. It is also a lot of fun on fine autumn afternoons, when the shadows are long and the light gone lazy. Here is a crash course (translated of tigers) in Feng Shui:

Go to the place you are interested in; front porch, building site, whatever. Face south (if you're using a compass, adjust 17 ½° degrees left for polar-geographic south in Island Park). For the very most fortunate Feng Shui for that location you would like water in front of you (south) flowing away from you if it is a river, the highest ground on your left (east), the lowest ground on your right (west), and a gentle slope up and higher than you behind (north). That's it (as long as Mars isn't in the eastern sky before midnight, of course, in which case you might want to wait a few weeks before doing anything lest the Peacock of Doom come visiting). If you find all is not as it should be, a good Feng Shui Man can adjust and tune-up the area by discreet planting of trees, or placing of bird-baths, or arranging of stones, or even driving rods into the ground (remember acupuncture?). It is said the birth of many sons can be assured by simply facing the porch a few feet one way or the other. I have read no up-date on winning the lottery with Feng Shui, but there are endless variations to the theme, of course.

My old Feng Shui compass was in the box, an ancient and much used thing, a gift from my teacher, but still pretty with red and black lacquer, twenty-eight concentric circles packed with tiny delicate Chinese characters converging on a small compass needle that pointed south. I carried it to the porch of my cottage and adjusted it to the time of day and the season. The Henrys Fork flowed brightly away to the south and the Black Tortoise nested happily out of sight in the Box Canyon behind. The Azure Dragon slumbered in protection on my left and the White Tiger guarded the west. Though I had not done this operation when choosing Lesser Frogpond (there was some haste and hurt during that time) the Feng Shui was favorable, even grand. I put the compass aside and smiled at the gracious sense of it all.

A bright-gray chickadee came and landed by the black cat at my feet. I felt very fortunate indeed.

LANTERNS

There will be a bit of a moon this Halloween night, a sliver tucked up on its side into the night just after sunset, playing nod with the planet Venus and, if you peer very carefully on Friday night, tiny Mercury low on the horizon. This moon will be a slim lantern compared to last years: then the moon was nearly at full on Halloween and the light splashed over eighteen inches of fresh snow making the shadows fill with mystery, though no spookish menace.

There is very little menace in the mountains at this season and indeed the Halloween festival is my favorite of the year; the little thrills of the holiday shaking me loose from the autumn torpor of warm days and chill nights. The wood is nearly in at Lesser Frogpond and it is becoming one of those years when we escape the early pesky snows and deep cold and the happy vagabonds of summer have mostly emptied off the mountain and all is So Right with our world that the tiny goblined excitements are a welcome relief from the utter contentment.

The other night I went for a walk in the woods with no lantern except the faint glow of the Milky Way arching a trellis of white-rose stars overhead, the shadows soft and slippery at the edge of the trail. The flying squirrels reclaim the Box Canyon pines and firs from the summer visitors now and their evenings are spent masquerading as sprites and elves in the branches above the river. The squirrels are so tame (or perhaps indifferent) to humans that I have had one run across my shoulder while I stood quietly against a tree, the little shiver as exquisite a thrill as any Halloween spooking. The same night I walked into a large object masquerading as a moose; the firs are heavy in that place and the dark nearly complete, so I had reached out in the trail to hold a tree or stone, and grasped her haunch to the surprise of us both, and she turned with a mild snort, but was without calf or anxiety, and I snorted in return and backtracked without haste, and we shared the night apart. One should walk carefully in the woods on Halloween.

The Trick or Treat crowd becomes quite permanent at Lesser Frogpond at this time of year. The chickadees have returned from their summer in the deep forest and we have raised many generations of them so that they have become familiar and taken on airs, such as threatening to turn carnivorous and hobgobliny if not constantly provided with the finest of black-oil sunflower seeds and chunked peanut butter. When they have finally offed to bed nearby, the resident squirrels and skunks come calling for treats. One early winter I rescued my porch from nine skunks in two nights of live-trapping. I had thought I had one very persistent skunk (their costumes are cute, but similar) and did not realize there was a gypsy camp of them nested out in the aspen waiting for the day crew to leave. I hauled each of the nine of them, like a Halloween school parade, several miles up the road, but this year one seems to have found its way back; it probably has that keen skunk radar for a handout and shows no alarm as I step over it to leave the porch. At least, I think there is just one.

The squirrels have become a problem and turned my meager cottage into a haunted house. The old cat and I share a one-room cabin that is only fourteen by sixteen feet in outside dimensions. For some years a female red squirrel has come to winter with us in a cavity near the ceiling in the southeast bookcase. She had gnawed herself a private outside entrance near the edge of the porch and takes a maze-like route up the inside of the wall to her nest. It is charming, if somewhat untidy, to see the edge of her winter nest of peanuts peeking out from between the bookcase and the wall. This season, a flying squirrel (or perhaps twenty flying squirrels, for all I know) has established squatter's rights in the cavity above the northwest bookcase on the opposite wall of the cabin. Sometime recently the flying squirrel, who is nocturnal, discovered by scent or radar, the red squirrel's (who is a day creature) cache of peanuts. Several times an evening, the flying squirrel lurks forth from its den, noisily runs the windowsills all the way around the outside of the cabin, and slips up on Mrs Squirrel's slumbers to raid the treasure. This brings forth from the walls a pretty ensemble of shrieks and hisses and whistles, as haunting as can be. They scramble down the inside of the wall, fighting all the way, and then the flying squirrel is off and all the way around the cabin again, scratching his booty into place in his own north nest, and then it is quiet again for a while until the next raid.

One night I saw them tumbling around on the porch, the skunk nearby waiting for stray peanuts to fall out of the fray, all of them lit season-orange by the light of the evening's jack-o'-lantern. Happy Halloween to all.

THE FIRST STORM

It began to snow last week in Island Park, an old style big storm, the heavy cloud masses following-folding on one another, crowding into one great continuing snowburst against the highest mountains, a weather pattern as ancient as the mountains themselves. The valley filled quickly with storm and soon there was another world to change life into, a new bright world to play into, without ever leaving the old place and hearth. I looked out the window at at the knee-wading snow, more still falling, insistently falling with purpose. It is always for me a shock, a continuing pleasant astonishment. 'The universe is rhythmic,' said the old Greeks. The seasons turn one into another.

Even some of the old-timers were caught by surprise, by the weight of the storm. There have been many years of drought, too many years to let the planning mind hold well a scene so suddenly and functionally different. It is a time of infolding, the cabin seems smaller and the distances to woodpile and work farther. The emotions begin to nurse quietly at smaller sentiments and far memory. The passes often close during these storms, passes into the valley, passes into the heart. An interior banked joy lays down as softly as the snow.

This may be one of the last best places where there can be moments as quiet as those of a hundred years ago: an old cat and a good fire in the stove and, within reach, the un-read pile of books that has been building all summer. Mine is a road less travelled, some nights closed with snow. Lesser Frogpond in winter is place where I may have the long times I require to think things out, only the song of the owl out in the silence.

She came to my cabin, again, under a full moon, again, with the snow still fresh and filled with light, the last of the storm still excited in her eyes. It was her first big storm in the mountains, I think, and she was full of breath and fast chirping words:

I would live like this, she said. I would have life like this. I looked her over; she was flushed with the cold and soaking wet from wading the snowfields to my cabin, her voice raw with rapture. She will do, she will do very well, I thought. I said:

It will lift you, this place. Frighten you and fill you, shock you and please you in the ways you have read about in the old books about other times. If you can live like this: alone in a place of your own, without bother or phone, moving about only at the convenience of the storms, the wild only one wall away, staying as strong as the cold and close stars; if you can live this way, I said, tied to the wings of your dream for the winter, you will purchase a great treasure for your own. A thing too rare in our time, a thing so simple and rich that it can be shared but never taken from you. A thing of your own.

She took a place by the fire and put the cat in her lap and waited. I said:

I think there were once more of us, folk who live in a happiness of too many words and scribble them away for a living. We will live just a little as they did, in our mountain fastness, a solitary trade in a solitary place. If you work hard and do your very best in this place, and can hold your dream warm in the storms, and you have tasted each moment of winter, the mountains will gift you a way of feeling both ancient and dear, an emotion deeply buried in our heritage but now long lost or weakened in other places. One day you will open your door and find the treasure arrived your porch.

Moonlight and wind turned at the door outside and she waited, having learned patience and attention from her first storm. I said:

Spring.

WINTER

The deep cold began last week in Island Park, the below-zero kind that gets inside me, that I can feel coming, the kind of cold that convinces my chemistry that winter has arrived.

The wind came skulking out of the north last Monday and I stopped what I was doing, without pretense or thought, and started stacking split stove-wood inside the only door of the only room of my small cabin. The old cat came in and started rearranging the little corners to his winter likings. We have done this before and moved with a certain practiced ease. I no longer conciously remember how long I have been here, how many winters we have been here together, the old cat and me. I suppose that is good; that I would have to sit down and think about it to know how many winters have passed. I have used up all the counting fingers on my hands so it is not an easy thing, the remembering and numbering of years. There has always been winter and the cold at this time and I have always been here, so I do not need to remember those things since the mountain will tell me the time and the season and I will be free to think of other things like dry fire-light wood and skirting the outside walls so the wind cannot run or howl beneath the floor. It is as proper and timely as morning, this peasant's life, and there is no longer a need to count the years.

There are things only the heart hears. Just as a person becomes more conciously aware, more keen when in danger, there is a place in you that is deeply alert to a beloved and familiar surrounding, a home sense. The cottage and forest at Lesser Frogpond sound different in winter, the wind is cold and curves in from another direction, and there are no aspen leaves to tame it, so there is a resonance, a hollow to my home that fills with winter. There is a spot by the river where I can tell, while approaching unseeing, the force and fullness of the water, tell from the sound of the stones singing at the passing water, the falling water's sound. It is like that with the wind at Lesser Frogpond, especially in winter, the wind will tell the fullness of the cold. It is a thing heard just below conciousness, like the slow pulse in my arm, heard only by the heart.

After the wood was stacked and the cat nested, I moved to the new rattles and whistles in the walls and started chinking the cracks with old poems and small pieces of bright cloth so the winter orchestra could not crescendo indoors. I do not like the north wind and it does not like me, having tried to kill me a few times when I dropped my guard. The wind has a place and I have mine, but I will not room with it and I think it an especially cunning and terrible neighbor. I am a stiff-necked man but I will bend and go indoors from that wind; it is a bully and would take my warmth away.

The wind that brought winter will be with us through much of this holiday season. But it is a price with great reward for when the wind slinks off it leaves great beauty behind. I stood on the porch late Monday evening after the wind and watched the stars call on the treetops. An owl sang nearby, or perhaps on the next ridge, the air was too thin and clear to tell distance. The forest was wind-swept, snow-clean, pure brisk. I suppose I think I have always been here because I cannot imagine being anywhere else.

I said to the mountain night, and I say to you, thank you for letting me live here and abiding my peculiar ways and reclusive habits. My table is full.

SNOWSPELL

The last fortnight in Island Park has been one of those times you think it is never going to stop snowing. With a few brief breaks of twenty below zero, it has been snowing every day. Life begins to revolve around, and fill up with, snowflakes. You get a little dizzy after a while, a kind of vertigo caused by the swirling-flashing air and the shapes of things softening and changing under the snow. The woodpile slowly vanishes; into the stove and into the snow. The world folds in and everything becomes harder, the level of difficulty raised by the more narrow and deeper time.

I have seen Island Park winters like this before, but it was so long ago and I was so new to it then in those fresh years. I had never seen snow fall out of the sky until I was 17 years old, and when I came here in my 30's the novelty was still on the thing and my fantasy-wrapped mountain man image intact. There was a wonderful awe of impossibility to it all then: it was impossible that someone could lead any kind of normal life in a world completely filled with over-the-belt-high snow. But people did things, some of them marvelously more than normal. So I read and I watched and I learned to do some of those things and found the value in the challenge and self-responsibility. You take pride in knowing how to do things here; it is all so impossible.

But I have become a slothful dog. The drought years pampered me plump and lazy. Oh, there have been some wide-eyed screamer storms in the last few years, but none of this steady bury-everything pattern that locks you up a little closer daily. I sometimes peer through the curtains at the stuff like a tiny person waiting for the doom; there is a small terror to watching the world softly go away. It reminds you of where you really are: high up on the Divide, out near the edge of the planet. Strange things can happen out here.

I opened the curtains this morning and it was snowing lightly. I looked out to where Lesser Frogpond used to be and I made myself think of the very worst thing that could happen. The very worst thing I could come up with was that I could be somewhere else, I could not be here in my home in the volcano. I took some more aspirin to try and pull down an anxiety-producing fever from the flu, and nodded thoughtfully out the window at the hundreds of miles of snow. It made a rude enough sense to calm me.

There is a new guest in the cottage this season. It is a Muse Mouse, I suppose, since the old cat has tolerated its company and it has established a cozy nest behind a volume of Chinese poems in the bookcase beside the fire. The mouse is welcome and a light eater. The mountain often sends messengers in unlikely forms: during one of the big storms last week, when the entire outside world had disolved into a white cage, the mouse clambered up on the windowsill and looked out at it all. I have never seen a mouse sigh, I am sure of it. But this mouse sighed and then turned and sauntered by the cat, up the wall, and into its nest. I heard it stir for a few moments and then it was quiet. I got the message and climbed into the bed with the cat. It was all too impossible to worry about, and tomorrow is another day.

1993

A Break

Huzza! Gadzooks! Eureka and Hooray! Bright beauty finally remembered Island Park for a few whiles last week and pulled off of the throttle on that devil's-own low pressure system that has set up siege off the coast of Oregon and been starving us of melotinin and humor and other light-induced, pituitary-happiness chemicals. Sunday was a very sun-day and the clouds looked grand now that they had a background of blue to Monet the whole thing into art instead of the trepidation of endless grey and white we have been living in for weeks. The surrounding mountains appeared, white-crowned old friends not seen for too long. Even the birds bent their beaks into smiles in the sunshine. Like me, they unhuddled and spread up their attitudes in the flood of light.

The temperature leapt like a bird set free, up into the middle 30's, and the ice softened and sighed and began to fall away. Hope broke out the shovels and plows and we began to make order and sense out of our highways and homes that had been savaged in the chaos of the endless storms and cold. Paths and woodpiles reappeared, and here-and-there were patches of asphalt helping point the traveller, like thin game-trails, up the road.

A local wag allowed how when he switched around on his television machine, he saw southern California washing into the ocean, Salt Lake City buried up past its abilities, hysteria in the ice caves called roads in Idaho Falls, freezing sleet in Iowa, volcanoes going off in Columbia, Somalia, the rat Saddam (maybe) getting his rat's hindness bombed off, and IBM stock (an Americon icon) skidding for the ditch. Said wag said maybe Island Park was the safest place to be since nine trillion-jillion feet of snow was no stranger to our memory and at least we knew when to give in, dig in, and give up. We knew when not to try to win the fight of making life normal.

I thought the fellow had an admirable case of the cutes and clevers for someone chained up in the dungeon of mid-January, but I've learned to never think of Island Park as a 'safe' place—not in January, not even in July. Most of us will survive this winter, many of us will even enjoy it; but Island Park is not an emotionally 'safe' place to make a home. I have seen these heart-swelling breaks in the herds of storms before (though never one that took so damn long in getting here), and they set the blood rushing toward something between rapture and hysteria. But one of the prices (and prizes) of living in the mountains is that things will never stay the same for long. While the sun is out I have turned the calendar to the wall so that I may not be intentionally reminded that it is a very long shadow yet to the buttercups of May.

The other evening I thought about what the fellow had said while I was not watching a television machine. I think things that go on outside of Island Park—out in the Other World—are important because we are all clinging to the same seamless ball of skin, and when someone scratches an itch on that skin—no matter how far away, I will feel the effect—no matter how slightly. I am a nervous enough man about the foilbles of my own species kin to want to keep track of things.

But this evening the cat and I went out onto the porch and watched the last afterglow of a seen sun fall darkly into the west. Turning east, I watched meat-red Mars rise in opposition. The ancients (and me) believed Mars to be a malevolent light, especially when in opposition to the sun. Mars was the yard-bully of the planets, the disturber of affairs, the bringer of wars and storms and terror. Perhaps it is not so much the generator of those things as it is the blood-red vampire that robs us of our strength to deal with life's normal calamities. It is a ancient and elegant excuse, anyway.

I looked out over Island Park, the mountains sleeping quietly under a thin moon. Lesser Frogpond was as hugely soft and radiant now as it had been hugely fierce and malicious a week before. My back and neck relaxed for the first time in weeks and I felt safe for not being in charge of all those changes.

I winked at meanie Mars, and the cat and I went in to our bed.

NEW WORLD IN ONE WEEK

In the early May of 1983, on a Wednesday, it snowed 18 inches, adding to an already hefty pile that lay lurking on the mountains and valley floor. The very next Wednesday it turned 80° and the stubborn snowpack melted as fast as the Wicked Witch of the West, the water coming down all in a rush, an ungraceful hurry so rapid that I watched live large-girth Douglas fir trees sweep past in the river at Last Chance, torn out of the Box Canyon by the fierce flow spilling out of and over the dam upstream.

Two weeks ago, in the early May of 1993, I pulled back the curtains to see it had snowed nine inches overnight on the still-remaining several foot base, and I despaired. Winter had come at Thanksgiving; it never stopped or relented; and I looked out the window at the same vast grey-white sameness I had been looking at for months and despaired of it ever changing.

Last week the temperature suddenly hit the high seventies and stayed there, day after day. The witch melted, and today there are violets and trout lillies in the yard at Lesser Frogpond, warm green grasses bursting out for barefoot afternoon walks. The frogs sing in the evening in the swale below the cabin, keeping rude harmony with the late calls of the sandhill cranes and the owl-like song of the mourning doves. A river ran across my road racing to a small waterfall in the swale, now a pond playground for the frogs and small ducks. All in a little over a week. I cracked the window open at night for the first time since last summer so I could sleep to the music of my new river and the soft sounds of a spring that was nearly already summer.

It was a long winter and strange. Dark. The '82-'83 winter was deep (though not as deep as this year) and the snow lasted into

May, but there were glorious and clear-sky breaks between the storms. We had days to spend out playing in the sunshine and good nights by the fire at 50° below listening to the old dead lodgepoles crack open in the cold and watching the stars hang at the edge of the window. This winter the sun abandoned us. From the first of December until this week there were less than twenty days of sunshine and no long periods of deep cold, just clouds and snow, sometimes a lot of snow, sometimes just nuisance flaking, but day after day of feeling caught in a narrow horizontal band between white and grey. Cabin Fever jumped up a few notches into sullen melancholy and a cranky looniness. I now find myself stepping carefully around the buttercups and violets in my yard because I had not realized, through all the drought years, how much I treasured them when their time came to my home.

I am a mostly-steady, plodding sort of man, the type that hates change and surprises. I am also a fool, because during a looney period I discovered that it was the drama and sudden changes of Island Park that had brought me here, kept me here, planted and nurtured my heart here. It was the darkness and sameness of this winter that drove me and others into a crushing, snappish ennui. It was an emotionally tough winter—not a physically harsh one—where the boredom and lack of challenging and changing weather and ways made us each our own enemy.

Island Park is not meant to be a graceful place. There is grace in the casting of a fly rod or the powder-swoosh of cross-country skis through the forest, but those things happen in this place and are not of it. The brutal ballet of the elk in autumn, under the golding aspen, is powerful and grand, but *graceful* is not the word for even that primal dance.

The majesty of these mountains is in the sudden and dramatic changes: winter to summer in a week, winter storms so violent and consuming that the blood runs a little colder from the howling wind, screaming with snow. There was thunder and hail this week that shook and pounded at the cabin and then sudden sultry sunshine an hour later. We are grateful for the water, but it is very much and has come very fast, and the run-off is not graceful. Even the violets are hasty and haphazard in their coming.

And so it should be, and finally is again: Island Park at its dramatic best. Life must be lived *large* here in this place too full of vitality and gumption to be *graceful*. I am a slow stump of a man, best suited to splitting wood and infinitives, and well-made for walking into sudden wind and bullying through storms. I shall never stubbornly wish for the security of sameness after the tedium of this last winter.

This morning, an osprey flew over the cabin carrying a trout almost as long as itself. The river is full of water and fish, and I feel myself filling also with the sudden changes. Next week, as the new aspen leaves unfold, I shall unfold my fly line out over the record-breaking running river, and give thanks that things are back to not being normal.

A Line To Ourselves

It is common notion that fishing is a quiet pastime, benign of strong emotion, another small trail to serenity. From Huck Finn to Hemingway, a picture emerges of humans slowly watching over the water, peaceful, fooling every so often with the rod and line more out of serendipity than seriousness. Fishing lacks the lust of the hunt, where the senses become so sharp that a keen tension drives the body and mind tight. Fishing is not a team sport, so there is rarely the pressure of contest, the need to prove or show.

One of my favorite pictures is of our columnist, Mike Lawson, standing wader-waist deep in the evening river, a fast riffle on one side of him chopped gold in the fading light, the other side a silver mirror of quiet water. Our mountains are behind him, shadowed tall in the twilight, and his rod is just coming forward, the line played out in a long omega loop, the fly coming gracefully past his arm, off to fetch the hint of a fish rising downstream. It is a calming picture, not one of those sports action photos with a leaping, mad-caught trout trying to bend the rod in half. The picture of Mike is simple—the man, the mountains, the river glorious with evening-glow, the small dark line looping out towards a small dark circle in the water. There is an ancient and comprehensible balance to the scene.

We have been going fishing for at least 45,000 years, to judge from some of the primitive (but not so different) hook artifacts found in archaelogical sites throughout the world. But surely it has been longer than that; fish are food and food has always been valu-able to us. A man gone fishing may find other nourishment also, something to still the mind and rewind the soul. There has always been stress—especially in the last million years or so that we have become awake to ourselves—and so perhaps we have always been fishing, have always all those years found this thing to soothe us. A line back to ourselves.

Here in the mountains fishing takes on a special quiet passion. Some of it, I think, is the grandeur of scenery surrounding: it is a big rough place set hard against a large sky, big fish and large moments lying just at hand. An ancient pastime in an ancient place that can let you touch old steady things in you that are difficult to reawaken in other places doing other things. There is the rapt anticipation of the rod taking life, an infatuation with the possible moment, as sweet and innocent as young love. The line falls on the water carrying a hope and—if we are gentle and do not get careless—the line returns a rapture and focusing enthrallment. A line back to ourselves.

Perhaps it is the same for other fishing styles, but I can only speak from the passion of my own ways. I never fish from a boat or the bank anymore, I am distracted by the bushes and bulwarks, and the meditation seems wrong and confusing. I am a simple and blunt man and require simple surroundings to get things right.

I step into the stream or some quiet corner of the river slowly, adjusting to the chill coming through my duct tape-patched waders. The rod is carried across one arm, like a scepter, like a wand. I'll find a spot fifty feet or so from the bank and jam my old boots into the slippery rocks on the bottom, locked against the flow, watching the water. Very often, almost always, the magic slowly begins and I feel my blood slowing and quieting, tuning to the moving water's pulse. When my eyes have cleaned my mind of everything but the river, the ritual begins. Like some ancient priest going through set and faith-full postures, I reach down with my left hand and begin pulling line from the reel, swinging the rod gently to pull the line through the guides to casting length. I feel rather than see the fly, always the same fly: a #10 Caddis in a light pattern, ugly and moth-like and easy to see on the water. When the line achieves geometry and grace, I put the fly down at the edge of a riffle. That is all there is to it, a ritual of cleansing because of its atavistic simplicity. Sometimes I catch fish and we act out an ancient dance before I release it or shake it off. Sometimes I just watch the ballet of the fly, turning and floating at drift, calming a little more with each cast. Both will work.

I bring things to the river each time: broken hearts and troubles, sometimes a heart swollen with someone and the joy being near them, failure and grief, small victories or the surprise of an unexpected kindness done me. It is a sharing: the water flowing around and in me, often carrying off the bad things for a while, often focusing and imbedding the happy feelings. I have gone empty to the river and returned full and whole. I have gone fishing bent down and beat up with burdens and come back up the bank lifted, shoulders up. Passion has many meanings: pain and pleasure, suffering and rapture; but the river accepts them all, makes the feelings true and simple, as the line singing out over the water brings me back to the real world and where I am in it.

I have sat by many a fire and listened this last winter. For many it was a difficult year, with disease and heartbreak, loss and too few options, the confinement of depression. A sad and difficult year. This weekend I hope we can find our way to the river—each of us has a river of our own—and heal our way into the coming season.

SHARING

Even for a hermit, there was a certain pleasure in watching the crowds that flocked to Island Park last weekend. There were herds of folks wherever you went, and almost all of them seemed to be having fun and appreciating the awed glee our mountains can bring. It was a slightly selfish pleasure for me because—while I find the bustle bothersome by temperment—watching them enjoy and use the beauty of this place reminded me of the first times I had come here and been moved to joy by this valley. That helped remind me to see the beauty a little better, and remind me of why I am still here, after all these years. Sometimes it helps to see things thought familiar through another's eyes.

For the visitors and pilgrims returning home, spring had arrived with perfect timing. We who were Winter Worn-Outs blithered that it was just three weeks ago that winter had gasped off, and they would nod their sunshined heads in sympathy and go off to watch the robins hatch or play with the big fish that seem to be everywhere this year. But watching them watch and splendor at the mountain's blooming lifted the winter off my back. I had been carrying the snow and dark too long after it was gone, and sharing the spring with others brought me up-to-date.

The weekend could not have been more perfectly orchestrated for the newcomers or those who had not been back for a while. The salmonflies were hatching on the lower river, and the fishing from Henrys Lake on down seems to be the best in seven or eight years. The meadows are blooming shooting stars and trout lillies and flaxen-yellow arnica, the brain mushroom crop is the best anyone has ever seen, and an occasional thunderstorm blew through to keep things cool and interesting.

I didn't even begrudge the big mosquitoes we haven't seen much of during the long drought years. 'Mosquitoes mean water and we've all been thirsty too long', a perfect stranger told me while he was slapping one the size of a small bird off his arm. I suddenly shared his viewpoint and smiled at the irony in his happy attitude. I also shared my repellent bottle with him, since sharing my personal body with mosquitoes is not a meaningful relationship to me.

I am ashamed that the years of daily familiarity with this place, coming on the heels of a tough winter, had made its beauty almost mundane to me, too unobserved and not gasped over by me, blinded by my dwelling on petty personal problems. Watching all the fun and pointing out of eagles and grinning on the man attached to a fish; watching all these others thawed my interior winter and reminded me that this special place was coming awake and alive, and I should do the same. At this time of the year I worship violets as a hobby; I have been much out among them since this last weekend and they are as worthy and inspiring as the very first ones I saw here all those years ago. I had somehow forgotten that I had come and stayed to live in the outdoors, and to let that help me live outside myself.

Partners and paramours, friends and strangers; we all need to see things we take for granted through another's eyes every so often to be reawakened and whole. I—who have all the arrogance of an independent recluse—must admit that maintenance of sanity and perspective require some contact with the rest of the tribe. I have shared often and well with the forest and the river, but they are of a different mind, and lack some of the quirky human qualities that should fill out a life.

Like lifting humor, for instance:

She has grown as lovely as one of my violets since I last saw her; a dark violet, black hair grown long now and framing eyes bark-brown and deep as our mountain night sky. She cocked her head at the jar of huge bright tulips I had given her. Little lines chirped up at the edges of her eyes and mouth. The flowers were very pretty and of many colors. I stole them from my neighbors, I said. Slunk them off for her, because they were so glorious that she should be holding them instead of the ground where they grew.

The lines deepened and the stars came out in her eyes, and she giggled merrily. Stolen tulips? she said. They are all the more beautiful for being wicked, and you are an odd man, she said.

I leaned back and laughed out loud for the first time in too long. We took the flowers out into the front of the office and shared the springshine and breeze. Perhaps it will be a good year, now that I can see again.

PAROLE

After a week of monsoon rains in Island Park, late last Saturday afternoon it began to snow. Real snow; October-like, stick-to-the-ground stuff, and the wind turned cold as a pagan's heart, rattling at the cabin walls at Lesser Frogpond, sneaking through the cracks and frosting my nerves. It just wasn't fair, I said to the cat, who reminded me that little in life is, and jumped up into the loft to bury his furry self in the old quilt.

My attitude went from morose to major snarly disgust. I pulled the curtains over the windows and then hung blankets over the curtains so that no light entered the little room: I had caved-in. I got the old stove huffing and puffing through the creosote and looked around for diversion. Out of hundreds of books on the walls, I could not find one I wanted to read. Out of a thousand literary chores, I could not find the bravado to tackle even one blank snow-white page. I went on strike. I turned out the only lamp and went to the corner chair and growled like a cur dog. After a while I thought I could hear the siren songs of fish and flowers outside, so I put a Bach funeral dirge on the tape player and turned it up loud. I could still hear the snow sliding along the roof. It just wasn't fair.

Sunday morning I crawled out of the sleeping bag, trying not to shake up the old cat who was inside tucked behind my knees, and pried back a bottom corner of the curtain-blanket to see if magic and prayer had transformed the world.

It had: the weight of sunlight about knocked me back onto the cat, who was now out also and chasing the skinny sunbeam I had made. I ripped the coverings from the windows and flung open the door. The snow had gone and been replaced by a be-jewelling fairy frost that glistened in the dawn light. It must have cleared during the night while I was in my cave, and the stars had come down to hang on the pines and foxtails. I jumped, bare as a crazed savage, off of the porch and out into the gentians and silver sage and looked all around. There was not a cloud anywhere. Not one. The frost nibbled at my knees, but it was already melting from night-magic to dew as the sun swung up the open path of the clear morning sky. Baby wrens and squirrels appeared from around the cabin and the yard filled with song. I could see the Tetons gleaming whitely off in the distance for the first time in weeks. Oh, happy bright June day.

I took coffee and cat out into the trees and listened to the new aspen leaves dripping the night off and opening to the warming sunlight. I hugged the cat, I hugged the porch-post, I got dressed and went out and hugged total strangers—who did not seem to mind and probably understood the rapture of a blue-bright June morning themselves after the suffering of snow the day before.

I went to a sunny spot across from the little waterfall in the Box Canyon and looked things over. A blue heron spotted me and honked, lifting as lightly from the water as my mood, and sailed gracefully downriver. A trout peeked around a log down below the canyon wall.

Having a life is complex, and that can be satisfying and challenging. Complicating that life into a problem is our own personal chore. Complexity outside, complications grow like some fey worm from the inside. A simple thing like a rainy day had been twisting my life for weeks. A simple thing like a sunny day had unbent that life. Mea Culpa.

I watched a water ouzel—a dipper bird—hop up the rocks and tuck its round brown body behind the waterfall. They make woven ball nests of moss and small twigs near running water and walk the bottom of the stream fetching caddis larvae from between the stones. It is a complex life for the little bird; touched by—but not ruled by—the weather. I have seen them busily doing the same thing I was watching when deep snow covered the banks. The ouzel can do nothing about the weather and so lives with it, not against it.

The complex, unpredictable weather of Island Park was one reason I had made a home here. I had forgotten that. Over 20 years ago, a tiny gentle man—a monk—had told me: 'Where there is no solution, there is no problem, only acceptance'. Obviously I had forgotten that also.

I got up, winked at the little bird and her waterfall, and went off to go fishing.

SHANGRI-LA

Most of the trees you see from the main roads in Island Park are lodgepole pine. Now, lodgepole is a fine tree, a useful tree, straight and strong, the wood ideal for building homes and fitting warmly into the stovebox. But it has the visual presence of a utilitarian, ubiquitous, slightly pretentiously tall weed. In other words, the lodgepole is a trifle boring. There is not much biological diversity in lodgepole stands: seen from above they look like an overgrown lawn with a few untidy wildflower-weeds mingled here and there.

Island Park is a hard topography to get to know; there are pockets of magic, small shy hidden areas that are filled with a kaleidoscope of living things. There are deer and bear in the meadows of the old-growth forest feeding on a varied banquet of plants and mosses, weasels nested sly and quick at the base of fir and spruce. Some of these holes of filled fir and and busy varied undergrowth are only a few acres, like the volcanic butte out near the end of Eccles road, where you walk from lodgepole and clearcut up a few feet into the fir and spruce and vines and the secretive dark monkshood—all fed by tiny seeps in the bearberry-covered lava. Raptors nest there and eat the bunnies and shrews, all within a small miracle of old forest. The headwaters of the Buffalo river are another niche in the ecology. You suddenly drop from the lodgepole down through a narrow bouldered gap into springs and spruce, the water slow and wide and shallow, filled with dancing watercress and bright brook trout.

One of the largest areas of old forest in Island Park are the Centennial and Henry's Lake mountains. They are a harbor of aspen and ancient firs filled with large, keen-eyed hawks watching the deer and elk and bear browse below. There was some timber harvesting in those areas decades ago, but much of that edge of the volcano has returned to or remained shadowed wild gardens. The last few years of drought were hard on these nests of water-loving areas; the streams dried up and the meadows dried out, and the old forests became home to dust and horseflies. This year's bounty of moisture has watered the gardens, and they are spectacular.

She took me for a drive this last week. She drove because she is wood-wise, born to back roads, and beautiful with independence of knowing what she wants and where she's going. She was looking for a flower, a rare species in this place, tiny and white and shy beneath the taller grasses. It is what she does, it was a quest. I was pleased she took me along, for I have been on quests for rare things before and understand pilgrimage.

We drove west, out past Sheridan, her strong hands quick and sure on the wheel, fighting the mud from the last night's rain. Then she turned off, up a canyon, and we rose up past a gap in the walls and came out looking out over a small valley of Shangri-La. I had been here before, but it was in the dry years, and now this pocket in the high hills had been transformed by the magic of water. The creek, normally dry, brooked through a meadow of camas and lupine. The old forest surrounding was mossy and verdant, and you could look up higher and see the new snow on the higher peaks all the way down to treeline. I felt restored and fresh, seeing Island Park as I had first seen it—with love and awe. She smiled my direction. There was no need for talk, for we have known each other's quests and things that swell the heart for some years now.

We stopped and got out, and went up the soft, saturated lush bench. After a few minutes of traversing, she bent lightly, black hair falling forward in wings, and reached into the dewed green grasses and spread them apart. She had found her flower. Her dark eyes are shaped like a doe deer, but are as keen as an eagles. I had not seen the plant, but she sees much that I do not. I stepped up into the firs and felt my pulse calm, the flow timing to the breeze and ryhthms of the place, cleansing me. It is peculiar, only the old forests or her company have ever brought me that sense of peace in the real world of present time. A calm Now, as simple and pleasuring as a cool drink of water on a hot day.

We drove back, she having found her rare flower and me, again, having found mine. She dropped me off, and I reached over and touched her hand and thanked her for the afternoon. It is the only physical intimacy I have allowed myself with her all these years; a touch and a shared smile fill my cup. You see, like the old forest, I love her too much and would not tamper with the specialness of either one.

JUST RIGHT

During my college years I had the good fortune to be on the east coast when one of the major museums was hanging a fine exhibition of Impressionist paintings. It was also a time when a scandal of forgeries had surfaced, occupying the media and the normally-insulated art world with what was genuine and how that affected value. I was young then, but not so young that that I didn't know that the idea of something being genuine was not just financial, but also metaphysical. I had not pondered the thing much—the young rarely do—until I turned a corner and found two Monet paintings hanging tightly side by side on the wall. They were not his later famous works of water lillies and his garden, these were a minor work I had admired in a book once: a crow perched on the railing of an old and crooked gate near a weathered wooden out-building, the bird looking away from the viewer down a snowy track into a thin tall thicket of leafless trees in the distance. A very haiku of a painting—but there were two of them.

I squinted at the small information plates under each one and was told that the one on the right was a forgery, a very good forgery it said. Like everyone else, I suppose, I leaned closer and saw the perfection of matching brush strokes and color-tones and signature of Monet. But when I stepped back so I could take in both paintings, I saw that one was right and one was wrong. I could find no single thing or technique that sent a false message from the copy, but it was there—somehow seen through the heart and not the eyes. The forgery was painted with a brush guided by avarice or arrogance, while Monet had let his anguish and aloneness reach out into the paint and canvas. Seen together it was obvious, though I could not define the particulars of why—one was sincere and the other an imposter, a well done mask of the other's honesty.

Most of our daily lives are played out in a Kabuki theatre of masks. Very little of the theatre is sinister or sociopathic. Most of the the posturing is required by the circumstances of modern life, where so much of our social contact is based on transactions—personal and professional—and where we are forced by practicallity or convenience to wear the masks of lover or businessman or friend. Often we become imposters of ourselves for noble and culturally correct motives: duty, obligation and responsibility, the wish not to inflict the internal chaos of being human on others. The ancients had carefully defined rituals to hold these roles bound in context, but now the masks are held firmly and habitually in place by the sheer number of transactions required, and perhaps that is why the tone of modern times is so cynical.

It is a gift of the mountains, this place, that a few feet off the road—like Alice and her Looking Glass—you can step through the postcard and into the forest that has such insistent authority of reality that it can compel some of us to respond in kind. Step through the postcard, out of the theatre, and the wind and bird-dance in the firs will make all masks useless baggage.

Last week, for a few days, summer in Island Park stopped being a forgery and turned warm and bright, the slow rhythms of mid-July meadows and streams replacing the storms that had been warring in the valleys and against the peaks. I fussed around the office with the puzzle of another newspaper, serene with sunshine, Mozart on the tape-player, the flies buzzing lazily against the warm glass of the windows.

An Alice stepped through the Looking Glass into the office. I turned and felt a sharp shock because I recognized her—though I had never seen her before—recognized her in that same indefinable way I had recognized the real Monet years before. She was a woman of no years, neither young nor old, having come ripe well and gracefully on her own terms. No mask, just eyes the color of grouse wings and tousled hair and fine skin the soft hue of new-pine bark. She stood as calm and unpretentious as the forest, as beautiful and serene as the summer day.

We transacted some small business and began to chat. She was a writer, a novelist, come here to Island Park to finish another book, home and husband and family in a neighboring state; she nested on family property here. She talked about her love of these mountains and meadows and the transforming inspiration they brought her. As we talked her eyes flickered and twinkled as her mind made the image-shaping leaps that writers can share. I began to recognize some of my own words as she described her love of Island Park; the images were not reflections of my words but a copacetic melding of companion emotions. She was alive, not just living, but alive with the mountains.

She laughed, as gaily and politely as a brook, at one of my stories, and then began to describe a magic place she had found—just right—in the Box Canyon, where she could sit on the cliff over the river and write for hours. I looked at her fawn-brown eyes and saw the rapture of someone else who had stepped through the post card.

I swallowed hard to suppress the small chimes and bells coming into my throat, because the spot she was describing is near my home, and where many of these columns have been written. A sprite piece of me from some deep well reached across the room and bonded with this woman of the woods. Our woods, our forest, though I did not tell her so because her life was full enough without my imposing the knowledge of our sameness to her. She was a companion to this place as I am; and for a brief time there was a genuine mating of moments, companions to each other through shared commonality of love and vision.

And then she was gone out the door, as quickly and quietly as a deer slipping into the trees. I went to a window opposite the door and looked up into our mountains. Perhaps she will come back again some day to chat, but it is enough to know she exists, that genuine sharing without imposture is possible. It was just right.

I went to a meadow that perhaps she knows also and did not feel alone and lay among the lupine and felt my heart begin to heal. She was as sincere as Monet's painting, no copy, that bright-brown woman, and on a summer afternoon she had made me feel whole.

A SHADOW OF SUMMER

To have peak-blossoming snows and dawn frost in Island Park in July is unusual, but not unheard of, even in my time. It is a price of homing in the mountains to sometimes have weather as sharp and difficult as the valley walls of the volcano we live in. We are high up at the edge of the world, out on the rim where the winds mature and grow strong, where the storms come calling and are caught and held by the crests of the Divide, and find turning to their purpose easy in the thin yielding air. This has been a shadow of a summer so far, pale and chill often, but this place takes what is offered, shadow and water, and has done well, grown and bloomed, deep roots of memory telling it how to adapt to the fickleness of the seasons.

This last Monday morning there was a heavy frost, the kind you scrape things from, a clinging chillness at sunrise that properly belongs to late September. A friend came to the office and said she had just, just barely, felt like she was recovering from being brutalized by last winter, and the frost frightened her and turned her mid-July thoughts to getting the wood in, something many have begun to do in fact. I told her the morning had chilled and alarmed me also, who had not suffered last winter well and was not full shed of the memory. One day at a time, dear poetess, I said. We choose to live here but often have little choice in the demands made by being out on the edge. I showed her the aspen leaves, so strong and thick-ripe with water that the frost had not pestered them and they showed no sign of the gold they would become. Do not buy the uncertainties of tomorrow by hostaging today. Accept this day here high up, as you have accepted so many others, I said, and tried within myself to do the same. Like my daily arguments with God, I said, you will always lose if you cannot accept what is offered out here at the edge.

And the day warmed and the chores fell away with the hours and I went deep into the forest where the shadows live to see what they had grown.

The herbs are out and the huckleberries are greening on the branch. Below in the lower valley, the domesticated crops are struggling with this thin summer, but the wild things of the woods are accepting and adapting with that risky freedom to change that wild things have. The deep forest is swollen with growth, and I set about gathering the harvest in the shadows: mint for cough and stomach, and to dry and place near the many gaps in the walls of the old cabin at Lesser Frogpond to discourage the white-footed mouse from slinking inside to nest warm; coral root and scullcap for the nights when the dragons come out to play and a strong tea of the dried plants will lull both them and me to sleep; mullein and aspen bark and red willow for winter's fevers and congestion; the rare and smelly valerian root that hides at the base of old pines and will relieve distress and the quiet the goblins of a troubled mind.

The deep forest is a secret garden and the shadows of the firs began to whisper to the shadows in my mind, whisper memories of once showing her the bounty of wellness that lives in the wild plants of the high, deep woods. The yarrow is tall and thick this year, the bright white flowers and feathery leaves showing up well among the grasses and gorse. Yarrow is perhaps the most common and most useful of our summer herbs. Yarrow will break a fever, I said to her, and clean the blood and quiet the nerves. I pulled a tall bunch and tied the base with loop of twine while she knelt in the soft spaghnam moss (an antiseptic) and watched.

Yarrow is most handy, I said, when the wind dies and the bugs come looking for the scented warmth of you. Crush the leaves and (especially if combined with common horsemint) rub the juice on exposed areas and it seems to trick the beasts away. Once bitten, chew the leaves and immediately apply the poultice and the sting and swelling will go away.

Before I could warn her, she swept up a handful of leaves and put them in her pretty mouth. Yarrow is a very bitter herb and her face tightened and shrank into a pout as the taste watered her eyes. She pulled out the stuff and placed it on her brown arm where a mosquito had been feeding sly a moment before. Her face brightened as the burning of the bite faded away. Without being told, she reached for a few leaves of my gathered mint and sucked on them to take away the bitterness. She smiled with the delight of a child's discovery, and her eyes bloomed a quiet light as she looked across the shadows at me. I suppose I blushed with the pleasure of her looking, and we gathered up the bundles of plants and started out of the forest, now grown July warm, a summer afternoon in Island Park. As I followed her, I saw her walk differently now than when we had come into the forest. She saw things and stepped around them, her tread as light as a deer. This place could change her, I thought, as it changed me. She could change me, I thought, for I was already a better, more happy, person for her brief company during our simple and ancient quest for plants. She belongs here, I thought, as she touched a gnarled old aspen, carressing the tree in passing. But I did not tell her so, or try to convince her to stay in the forest and make a life.

I think she knows that and there will come a season when, as I once discovered so many years ago, she will not be able to leave these mountains. We stepped out of the edge of the forest and the shadows lessened. Many shadows lessened. Summer was with and within her.

An Armful of Sunshine

Summer arrived fashionably late to the party last week in Island Park. The old cat seems to think it will last and has made an afternoon nest in the woodpile on the porch at Lesser Frogpond, tucked into the old flannel shirt I use when working out in the trees. The sego lillies, a sun-loving beauty of a blossom, erupted out everywhere this week, and that is a good sign of holding weather. Even the house squirrels have moved out into the warming forest.

I think perhaps 1983 was the last year I remember seeing our high valley so filled with green and glorying things. There is the sharp sweet smell of chamomile underfoot as I move across the yard from cabin to truck, and mint in the swale comes soft and subtle through the west window in evening when the high sun warms the rock cliffs they shelter in.

And now we have the high sun, late but welcome, and a forest freshened up after the drought years, and the combination has once more revealed how light at this altitude can produce hues and shades that are deprived those who live in lesser, lower places. Maxfield Parrish painted skies like ours; deep pastels between the fluffed-up clouds, and Turner and Constable caught the deep magic of colors in a shadowed grove. We are closer to the sun, we who home on the edge of the Great Divide, and that can change the light as it slides off the canyon walls or slips through the trees touching the wild roses and pale geraniums; sometimes that light can change your vision, or even your life, if you go out to participate in the feast of high summer. This is a fine time to be in such a fine best place like Island Park, and I am grateful with awe.

'Spirituality' is a much over-used and abused word in these modern times, but there is a possessing spirituality about the light in the high mountains in bloom and leaf. I am a plodding sort and jealous of my own company, so it has taken me many years to begin to learn how to share that awe-swelling with others. I have had to learn to curb my pompous chattering ways—pointing out this and naming that—when out in the wild with another. Sharing is not lecturing; it is taking them to a special place and standing by to quietly watch them find their own special way to belong there.

Last Sunday I took a friend high up to a place where the partridges and columbines play. She had never been there, as have few others—the road is sly and narrow and steep and impossible in the wintertime, even for snowmachines, and the place so hidden that the sky keeps its secrets and has allowed the forest to grow old in quiet peace. I tucked the truck in a tangle of gooseberry vines, opened the door for her, and let her roam.

She immediately saw the clear difference in what the high summer sunlight can transform at nearly eight thousand feet. She stood in a small meadow and looked out over the lake to the west, and then down the lupined valley to the south and over at the nearly full moon coming up the backside of the mountains in the east. The breeze and light touched her hair and eyes, and she smiled and smiled and smiled. I stood near her and slightly back, sharing the adoration, needing to say nothing. She is as special as the place, and it belonged to her before the shadows had moved the length of her brown hand, a hand she used to stroke and then embrace the rough bark of an ancient Doug fir, peering at the holes and snags that held the flying squirrels and raptor nests.

She cooed over larkspur in the open and moved to find their subtled purple-blues in shadow. She carried columbines in and out of the trees, the colors of the flowers and the color of her eyes changing as she moved like a fawn from place to place.

The sunshine is so different, so strong even in shadow here, she said. Yes, I said. I don't want to go back down, she said, clutching the flowers and turning them in her eyelight. I smiled and nodded, holding out a palmful of wolf moss, turning it from pale green to deep blue as I turned my hand. She looked out over the lake and said: It is not that there is anything wrong down there, it's just that it is so special up here.

Yes, I said. There are special places down there also. We make them so by seeing them in true light.

I took her up the mountainside to show her the game trail running thinly along the ridge deep in the trees. The Doug fir are thick there and it is dark. I put my arm around her to steady her on the narrow trail as we stopped to look down at the tracks of the large ones who live here. She turned her head up and looked at me and lightly touched my hand, and the color of her eyes changed though there was no light here to do that. She had her own lights within and I held an armful of sunshine in her, and I blushed and looked away. She touched my hand again, and then I took my arm away and led her out into the sunshine, now cherishing the rising moon, and took her to the truck and back down.

I did not tell her, for she already knew, that if I did not take her away then, on that high summer afternoon, from that place and the lights, that I might not find the strength to leave her. There or anywhere.

PERSEPHONE IN FULL BLOOM

Summer was in the mountains this week, mature and come full ripe. The mornings dawn-ray misty and cool, the days mostly clear and of a considerate and comfortable temperature, and the storms were polite enough to hold off till evening, quick and showy, gaudy lightning and thunder at the window of the old cabin, a lullaby of wind clearing the mind for sleep. Though it was late in coming, the season has matured rapidly, caught up to it's August coming of age.

The flowers are happy and numerous both in quantity and diversity, the fish still roll up to the call of the line cast across a full and filled river, and the young raptors are out of the nest and tumbling the afternoon wind with coltish clumsiness and charming curiousity over anything from bugs to voles that might want to play for dinner. The blooming fireweed and crisp smell of the morning's chill dew are signals to summer's peak and harbingers of the autumn soon to come. But were there no other sign, no other omen or portent, just the color of the aspen leaves come green-grown dark would be enough to tell the ripening of summer: the aspen leaves have turned the color of Persephone's eyes.

The old Greeks had fun making myths and turned it into high art, which it is. Their myths were taken to extremes so they might be rich with complexity yet concise. We live in a place of extremes and this place is well given to the old stories. Persephone was a maiden captured by Pluto, the king of the lowerworld, and tempted to eat just a few bites of persimmon fruit in that dark place, and so was compelled by her persimmoned promise to remain in the lowerworld and honor and love her king. But Persephone was also summer in her person, bright and warm and gay, and the gods grew tired of the year-long dark and cold and plea-bargained an agreement that allowed her to emerge into the upper world for half the year, before returning below to her king of shadows.

She often comes to our mountains late and leaves early, for this is a high distant place we live in, and she must travel far. The myth may seem a primitive and simplistic explanation of the seasons, but it is satisfying and personal and can humanize nature in a way that let's us share a wild harmony with the orchestra of leaf and branch and changing sky. It is a story of growth and coming full and exile and rebirth: Persephone comes to us young in the spring, impulsive and unpredictable as a child-woman set free, with the self-indulgent temper to match. But now, in August, she is grown and at comfort in the forest, and has aged wise and well. She shares and imparts to the mountains at full bloom that complicated, fascinating beauty that only the mature have. It is the gentle, strong confidence of coming of age. When she begins to leave in the fall, the elk will grow wild with need and the grasses will grow dry of their blood sap, and the forest will boil with passion; the aspen turning hot gold, the evenings turning to musk and moonlight and haunting songs of owl and elk.

She does not come back in winter—our thaws are merely memories and daydreams of the air. I will keep her tokens near me through winter; now is the time of herb-gathering and soon the berries. But she will not be here as she is now: Persphone is called by something greater than her or us, beyond her and us. Duty and obligation, queen of the seasons and giver of what is timely and proper.

This personalization of nature's metronome, however fanciful, helps us with the harsher tyrannies that can come in this extreme place. To love these mountains and what they bring is to love Persephone and the hope and longing that love brings. To see things through the kaleidoscope of myth and still stay grounded enough to fetch the wood and water in blizzard wind, can bring health to the attitude.

Recluses and writers are a fanciful bunch of fools, of course. The mountains are a good place to set them and their ravings as protection for the general public. But this summer I believe I met Persephone in the woods, just a glimpse now and again, a fully mature aspen-eyed beauty, bringing warmth and flowered-laughter to this high season and the wide valley I call home. One evening, just at twilight, along the Box Canyon I may have even heard her voice in the muttering water and whispering leaves, heard her ancient promise that will echo through my winter. She said: I will leave because I must, I will return because I must. Persephone's promise made in full bloom.

ONCE IN A BLUE MOON

This Tuesday morning last, the old cat and I kicked the coffee machine into gurgling submission, checked the thermometer (17°) and decided that was nothing fatal or fearsome, and took our respective places out on the porch at Lesser Frogpond and wondered what the poor folk were doing.

That may sound strange coming from two furry creatures who have essentially been camped out in the mountains for most of a dozen years or more without refrigerator, running water, or cooking stove. But there it was. The porch looked over riches beyond a wildest wish of wealth.

The frost was rising in the dawn light into a soft mist in the golding aspens. Rising sharply above the fingers of white wisp were the tips of the Tetons, clear in the cold, and a blue moon was setting plump in the west, rolling down and over the Continental Divide. The coffee tasted sin-black fine, and the cat eyed a morning chipmunk with regal disdain. It was as fine a morning as the mountains offer, and we were kings of the porch. 'Once in a Blue Moon,' they say. Not here. Not at this edge of paradise. These mornings are often and welcome here and make the heart rich.

The origins of 'Once in a Blue Moon' seem to be lost in the fogs of history, but currently it means two full moons in one month. That won't happen again until the last day of June, 1996, so it has come down to us as meaning something rare. Rare, maybe, but a little dry—being a trick of the arbitrary calendar—for this old mystic. I have seen three blue-colored moons: one in Winnepeg, Canada when I was playing guitar on the road too many years ago to remember the date, one during the Yellowstone Fires of 1988, here, when the moon rose meat-red in the smoke and pulled out blue at the edges as it climbed further, and one in August of 1991, briefly blue, probably caused by the smoke of the eruption of Mount Pinatubo in the Philippines, half a world away.

It does not, for me, decrease the awe caused of such an event by knowing the reasons behind the phenomena, the magic of this place overwhelms the science. Things as rare as a Blue Moon are common and often here for those who look to see and notice. There is much wealth of things not normal in Island Park.

It is a wealth to be shared, and I hope that the weather of warm-ish days and cold star-sharpening nights holds as predicted, so that the holiday visitors this weekend can share the treasure. If only a few of them tuck away the memory of the mountains in autumn and carry it away home with them, to bring out and dream over in other times, I shall be grateful that they have been given a piece of what we who live here have daily. I think it helps folk who must live in other places to know that the magic of the mountains really does exist. It can keep one balanced against harm to know such things are real.

Sharing sets the seeds of love, and there are many who love this place, especially at this time of the year when the 'season' is sup-posed to be ending, but can be the finest of all times here high out on the edge.

I took a long walk out into the evening monday night, for the simple pleasure and duty of living here at this time. Far down the road I passed an older couple on their east-facing porch and waved. I have seen them for years but do not know their names, nor have ever spoken. They are homebodies like myself, I suppose, and do not need or seek idle chatter on such nights. The evening was young enough to be chill without being cold, and the twilight held the pastels of the meadow flowers and the track of old road. The couple were holding hands watching the nearly full blue moon rising, and before they spotted me padding down the road, I could see them look at each other often and smile, saying nothing, not needing to say anything. Good, solid, paid-your-dues love under a swelling moon.

I waved as usual in passing, and they smiled and waved as usual with the hands that were not holding each other. Farther down the road I felt the twinge of being alone, a little jealousy maybe, envy maybe. What would I, with all my wealth, trade for a hand to hold, I wondered? Why, nothing of course, whispered the aspens. It cannot be bartered or bought or sold, smiled the moon. The hand must be given, not taken, to have what those behind me on the road share.

Perhaps some day, some other blue moon, the old cat and I will move over a little in the cabin to make room for another. Someday, perhaps. Now I am grateful for the moonlight in my hand and a land that is my home and shares so freely of its gifts.

ORDER OUT OF CHAOS

The cold has come. Not the nippish twenty-something stuff; the real down in the teens, bite your nose, frost your windows, cat stays inside-type cold. The pilgriming clouds no longer look like shape-making summer fantasies; they've taken on a ponderous, edged and serious-silver look. The moon is dark this week so I have to make my way to the little out-building at Lesser Frogpond at night by the sound of the crunch underfoot: this crackle for foot off the trail and in the stiff weeds, that softer gritch for when you have found the trail in the dry carpet of chamomile. This kind of cold turns the mind from sloth and convinces the attitude that the time for planning has come.

I hear the *Old Farmer's Almanac* is out and calling for a mild winter for our several-state area. Phui. There is no such thing as a mild winter at this altitude, this close to where the weather scamps play. Winter is the season of chaos here; each day—or even part of a day—unpredictable and surprising. Sometimes astonishing. Temperatures can swing 60°-80° in a twenty-four hour period and an unexpected storm can sneak between the peaks of Sawtelle and Jefferson and catch you in your shirt-sleeves, running out of the forest for the shelter of the cabin, the wind and snow at your back hurrying you right along.

Getting along (and enjoying) this season of chaos requires that things be put in order around the estate. What can be seen plainly out the window on a morning may go into hiding under a cloak of snow by afternoon, the memory of the tool, or woodpile, or truck, fading quickly in the white shapelessness of a new geography you hadn't planned on for that day.

I have seen soft autumns where I grew languid and content on the porch, the song of the grasshoppers lulling me into an indolence that caught me off guard when winter arrived within hours, unannounced, of Indian Summer. Those winters were a puzzlement of hide-and-seek to determine which mound of snow hid the pile that had the thing I needed: maul, dinner, wood, cat, whatever.

This year I decided: no piles. Everything stacked and in its place. No more searches in the north wind and white-outs, I vowed. Order out of, and before, the coming Chaos. The wood is stacked and piled in little packages around the grounds: February-March pile here, March-April pile a little farther off, split and stacked wood nested on half the porch for Big Storm days, the porch screened off from the howler winds with sheets of plywood, the water jugs tucked inside their winter corner of the cabin to keep them from freezing and splitting in the star-bright cold, the tools oiled and ready to hand nearby, duct-tape (a necessary decorating commodity) blocking most of the cracks in the walls and corners and a fresh roll ready for when the winter wind choir starts singing in the gaps I haven't found. It is satisfying. Should the weather turn back to summer (ha!), that will be just fine, and I will still be able to look at the skis and snowshoes hanging on the wall outside the door with fondness.

There can be much fun in winter's chaos, often approaching rapture—if you are ready. Like my arguments with God, I have lost every fight I have ever had with winter in these home mountains and will fight no more. There is joy in the unexpected if you are prepared it; the simple happiness of surprise, instead of being beaten flat down and helpless. If you would live in the Elements, then make your life elemental.

She is like that. When we are together there is a happy chaos of conversation; tag lines put on sentences spoken hours before, laughter at the unexpected images we form and the subjects that storm through our company of each other. She is a wild one, not in the modern sense of something bad, but in the older more ancient ways of having a free mind and the simple trust to share that mind's playfullness. A chaos of glee between us, as strong and commanding of attention and gratitude as the relationship I hope to have with the winter coming. I shall miss her by the fire, the cat humming happily in her lap, but I will hear her laughter in the storms and talk about her to the stars that are so much like the ones in her eyes. I am ready.

VENUS'S HONEY

It is a happy time. The last three weeks or so are the first I have seen of Island Park in all its showy, gaudy, magnificently normal beauty since perhaps last Thanksgiving. It has been a strange year for weather and behaviour, all agree.

Some talk about summer finally having arrived, but I think to say so does an injustice, an insult, to our mountain autumn. It has simply been some years since we have seen enough of fall to be given time to overcome the shock of how grand this season can be. It is a time to be out and looking, recovering the love of place that a few lost these last dry years and last dark winter. Driving can be a little distracting right now: there are bright red mountain ash berries hiding like sprites at the edges of the road on the Ashton Hill causing some sudden lane changes for the unwary as they gawk out the window. Beauty can be dangerous and so compelling that you lose track of what normal, taken-for-granted thing you are doing. That is also one of Beauty's gifts.

Take a slow drive or stroll on any of the old side roads come evening and you will re-find Island Park as it is supposed to be at this ripened time. The thick crowds of hasty visitors have mostly made their way down off the mountain and left behind the quiet of the forest, the deer returning to the roadside red-ripe willows, and small rattle of the little ones making their whiskered way through the dry grasses, their pouches full of harvest seeds.

The moon is full this week, and if you wish to know how love appears, go out under the golden aspen and look up at the moonlight; how it makes the trees glow. The vision is alarming and awesome, like love, each leaf catching the magic of the silver light. I love the aspen and this place and this time. Not only has the heart come home, home has returned to the heart. No, this is not summer, this is just as it is supposed to be: autumn in the Rockies.

Last evening, after the cat and I had taken in our evening stroll on the old road near Lesser Frogpond, the cat humming down beside me in the moonlight (it is a happy time), we went home and I settled in front of the stove for some light reading. Lucretius lived from about 100 B.C. to 55 B.C., much of it in mountain places near Athens, where they have aspens and red-berried ash and dusty, quiet roads. He was trained as a poet, but his most famous work is called simply (poets cannot avoid pretense): The Nature of the Universe. Years ago, I was taught in college that the poor fellow lacked the instruments to measure things: thermometer, telescope, barometer and such (for the plain reason that they hadn't been invented yet), and that we should consider his reasoning about the nature of things literature rather than science.

Phui. That is a patronizing attitude I (now) think. The man was a poet and his observations are a wonderful tangle and confusion of metaphors and literary conceits, but the man could see well and reported honestly.

Before the fire, on an autumn-chill evening, the cat still humming beside me, I came across this from Lucretius:

"This, then, is what we term Venus [the greek goddess, not the planet]. This is the origin of the thing called love—that drop of Venus's honey that first drips into our heart… Though the object of your love may be absent, images of it still haunt you and the beloved name chimes sweetly in your ears."

I should have remembered that during the last dark winter when I was haunted by the absence of this place's grand beauty. Fortunately, its chimes—and eventually other music—brought my heart back home.

I put the old book down and went outside, down into the swale and under the trees. I looked up through the aspens at the nearly-full moon. Each leaf was a golden, glowing shadow. Each leaf was a drop of Venus's honey. I grinned to myself as I looked around to see if anyone was watching (sometimes love is furtive) and picked one of the honey leaves and scurried back to the cabin, an owl hooting at the greying thief who was stealing gold. I put the leaf in a little wooden box by itself and put it on a shelf.

The leaf will chime in the box come February and remind me of this special time. Or perhaps I will share it with someone special some other special time. Another poet once wrote that love not shared is an empty cup; beautiful but not filled or refreshing, not redeeming. Perhaps I can fill that cup someday with the bait of Venus's honey.

FROST AND FEVER

I was just fooling around the cabin Monday night, re-reading a tome on thirteenth century Europe which always puts me in a better mood, since the thirteenth century was an unspeakable time of brutality and feudal stupidity for our young species that puts our modern times in a better light and perspective. Their version of chivalry had a lot of Neandertal overtones, and what passed for religion during much of the century was two Popes stealing money from the peasants to build armies to fight each other and kill peasants. We are more civilized (or sly) now, aren't we?

At full dark I left the cabin for the short and familiar trip to the small out-building that houses Personal Business Headquarters at Lesser Frogpond. I was wearing only an old pair of shorts, the cabin being toasty, cat-curling warm from the little stove. I stopped on the way back to admire the moon rising behind the trees in the east, the silver light helping the frost begin to find the edges on the fireweed leaves and foxtails, little forking lines of ice, like white lightning, starting to form on the windows of the old truck. I grinned in the cold, happy to be here, Saturn burning yellow-bright low in the southern sky and white Jupiter falling away in the west.

Out of the west, out of the dark, from across the moon-sparkled wild river, came a keening, a rising scream carried by its own urgency on this night of no wind, a call as ancient as the stones, as old as blood.

An elk bugling. A big one. A song of challenge and lust that echoed down the centuries. It had begun.

I turned away from the cabin, grabbed some old mocassins out of the truck, and went west up the bench and into the trees, shivering in the cold. He sang again and I bent northwest, trotting now along an old game trail I knew, crossed the old road and loped to the river, my breath coming hard and visible in the moonlight and frost.

There is a place on the edge of the Box Canyon, below the waterfall on the opposite cliff, where you can look across the river to a meadow ringed by aspen and fir, an open clearing in the protected forest of Antelope Park, an arena, a staging area and stage for the high opera of autumn. Mist was beginning to rise from the river, wisps of water-warm ghosts given shape in the cold air, an army of vapors moving up the canyon walls and into the trees on either side. I stood on a lava ledge, under the moon and over the river, squinting out into the dark, one arm holding the twisted branch of a fir for support and the small wamth of the tree.

I was cold. Then the bull called again and I was not cold. Across the river, a few hundred feet away, he stepped out of the aspens and mist and threw his massive antlers onto his back, raising his head from swollen neck and howling a high whistle rising into a scream of demand. I felt a shimmer of sweat begin upon me as my pulse caught the cadence of the song. The mist caught a tiny breeze out of the west and brought me the smell of them, the musk, then I could see more shapes dancing lightly, ballet-slow, in the clearing. Cows coming to the call, drawn, compelled, to the edges of the arena.

Other bulls took up the chorus somewhere deeper in the forest and the old bull on the cliff across from me soared into madness and began tearing up the earth he stood on with his great antlers, grunting and growling. Like mine, his breath came visible and joined the army of mist. Like mine, I could see the sweat on his neck glimmering in the moonlight. Larger shapes, not cows, appeared at the edges of the clearing and our breath came faster, more urgent. I could hear antlers tearing at tree limbs, and I could hear my own heart pushing at the edges of my ribs. The old bull screamed under the moon again and I shivered in the heat.

Fever and frost. Blood calls to blood in this ancient drama. Somewhere rooted in the cells of all that wear flesh there is a kinship of fever that screams a challenge under the pagan October moon. The old bull moved to the center of the stage and took his ground. The breeze stopped and the army of mist multiplied in the frost on both sides of the river, hugging the forest and earth, gripping and shrouding the beasts on each side. I heard the sound of antlers crashing on antlers and found my arm and chest scratched and bleeding where I had been clutching the ragged bark of the tree, leaning too far out over the river. Too far out on the edge. Great horned heads lifted and fell in the mists across the way and the screams raised the hair on my neck and arms and belly.

I backed up and turned away, turned away before I fell too far into the dark. Turned away and went home.

In the cabin, the book on the thirteenth century still lay open on the arm of the chair. I splashed water from the bowl by the door onto me, to break the ice of my own sweat—formed on the trail home, under the moon, out in the dark. I closed the window to soften the sounds of battle across the river but it was a long time before I could soften the pounding of my own heart. I looked at the book on the history of our brutal century past, and understood them a little better. I moved closer to the stove as the fever left me and understood a little more of where I had come from and what I was.

SHED A LEAF, SHED A TEAR

There was fog this morning; not the summer-green smell of a mist that throws off the night and blossoms into a sun-swarming day—this was a clammy, clutching cloud of near-frost and old water, smelling of decay and empty trees. This kind of morning foretells a change in the weather, a change in the season, an awakening from a midsummer's night dream. The mountains have grown white-topped; old men mountains looking down into our valley, their breath full of winter.

Our summer weather (beginning in September) was so short and hasty and beautiful that the season was more bitter-sweet than usual; high value is always placed on things that are rare and infrequent. She had shed some tears on departing as we watched a cold wind pluck the aspens bare. It will never be the same, she had said. I sincerely hope not, I had said. It is the way of things here in the mountains to be different and change, I had said. This is the frontier of dreams, the place where chances are born. I would pull down this moon as a bright toy for you to play with, but I cannot. I cannot stop the course of the moon, or the course of the seasons, or hold the moment's plenty; I just live here, like the owl and the drying fireweed and the soon-sleeping mouse; I just live here always and cannot change the changes. Goodbye leaf, goodbye summer, goodbye good friend; may you find your own way well under another moon in another place. Everything will be fine, I said.

It was bravado, of course, for I cried also when she left, sitting in a withered bed of aspen leaves with the old cat, as the moon died on the western mountains, slowly dimming like a lamp going dry of fuel. The cat frisked an old pinecone in the last of the moonlight and I finally laughed, he stopping and looking over his shoulder at me with wise satisfaction. Yes, old friend, I said, let us go in and play before the fire and then I'll find a book of old dreams and the chair, and you the blanket near the stove, and wait until sleep visits us in the full dark.

Is it a tragedy when the last golden leaf of summer falls? Or the last osprey lifts from the nest and bends south with the wind? "Quo Vadis?" ("Where are you going?"), said the sacred stranger to Peter who was fleeing the death that awaited him in Rome. Quo Vadis? said the man to the last leaf of summer and the osprey growing tiny and then gone from sight over the crooked Tetons.

It is a tragedy to the man because we humans are prisoners of time, held hostage by the moment, too myopic and mortal to see the larger reality. It is an enigma that torments and confuses us.

Fortunately, here the mountains are close enough to touch, close enough to cling to and learn from. The mountains do not see the falling of the leaf with human self-serving drama. For the mountains, nothing dies or says goodbye; for the mountains there are patterns and cycles and seasons and 'forever' is a word not necessary to their being, not a wish they need to endure.

The leaf falls to become the soil that nurses the tree that grows the leaf again. And again, and again. Summer does not die into winter, it sleeps and renews and rests. Winter gives time and respite for the old to become new. The mountains know these simple, important things, and if I'm allowed to live long enough here perhaps I will learn their lesson.

Sleep well this winter, my princess of the moon.

THE LONG NIGHTS BEGIN

We are rushing to the dark these last weeks out on the northern edge of the planet. The pace at which the night conquers day increases at this season; we were losing three minutes of daylight each day a few weeks ago, and nearly four minutes now. It is more obvious lately, the day pinched between late morning and early evening, rising in the dark and finishing the chores by twilight, the shadows grown longer as the sun swings lower and infrequent. I am looking out the window at Lesser Frogpond at a three-day old moon, thin and cold-white against the naked trees, the full dark of night come at a time that was bright early evening three weeks ago.

And so the long nights begin. The solstice just before Christmas will mark the scientific time of the sun's return, but we are in a wobbly ellipse of an orbit, riding a bent planet at an angle to the light, a pilgrim planet with a limping, halting stride to summer, and we will not notice the lifting of the light until the first week in February.

And so the long nights begin. An owl sings softly in the swale outside the window, under the shy new moon, but there is no answering call. I can see its shadow on the end of a bare branch, cooing into the empty dark. The snow has not come yet, so the forest is even darker, abandoned of leaf and hawk, all flown south on the wind, the north wind that carries the dark here and carries the daylight away. The owl tries again, but it is the season of echoes, hollow of answers, the forest asleep and alone.

Perhaps I will go this week, go before I become petulant and angry of the dark, go up to a high place I have known where there are tiny lakes clinging like bird nests to the edge of the Divide, high up where it is steep and difficult, to a covey of pines that hug the mountain's top. You can sit in that place amongst them, cradled from the wind, and it is open and you can see as far as you are willing to see. It is very pretty there, a good place to be alone with yourself. Sometimes I have needed that high place to catch my breath and re-balance; like one of those old time iron-bar magnets that you had to pass through a strong energy field to get them re-polarized and pointing straight. Perhaps I will go there this week, though I really don't want to. I will go because of that.

There is difficulty: I am a little shy of the high places lately, there is so much up there and so much to come down from, and the way is difficult and strips you down in the getting there. I am a little afraid of the effort it takes to reset my internal compass lately. As I grow older, sentiment and awe have grown deeper and more rooted in my daily life, pride no longer a shield against the strong feelings, the devotions and adorations I wear like thick vines on an old wall. The plain emotions are so much more important now that I am more plain, less complicated by my own self-importance, all that torn away these years in the dark when the north wind comes. Love and sorrow, kindness and harm, the plain and direct passions of friendship and deep bonding; all these have taken on weight and meaning with the passing miles. I have been allowed the grace to care deeply and often about some things and some people, but I am hesitant to climb alone any longer to that grove of trees, so high up, where my memory can see as far as I am willing. I do not know whether I want my memory, honed and keen, as a companion during the long nights anymore.

The owl cries again, the pitch a little higher and more plaintive this time, and the old cat grows restless and paces at the door. We are not afraid of the dark, we three have been here many years under thin moons in empty forests. We are just moody and adjusting to how fickle the dark can be without company, it throws your own shadows back at you and calls up too many illusions between the trees.

I suppose I will go up to the high place because I need to get above the shadows and see well, see whatever is offered me, bind the true things from last summer's light to me before coming back down into the long nights. I need to wonder at and about things, separate the fact from the wish, and return grateful for what I have, free from wanting more, content with joys exchanged in the past light, and keep that my company for winter.

A shadow crosses the window. It is the owl carrying his cry away into the dark. I wish him well on his quest this long night.

WAITING

The wood is in and tarped down in graceful and strategic piles around the cabin. The windows are winter-curtained with see-through stuff lest the warmth go out and the dark come in to trouble the huddled wintering man and cat. The straw bales are against the outside walls, the outhouse is swept and stocked with this year's almanacs, and the stovepipe is clean and frisky for quick hot fires to take the frost off of fingers and tails.

So where's the Stuff?

I hate waiting. One of the many non-boring things about homing this high in the mountains is you never know if you are prepared until the event arrives. Right now we're running the pre-Thanksgiving race between which event arrives first: deep cold or deep snow.

I'd prefer the snow, first since the cabin at Lesser Frogpond was moved in haste and huff years ago and never jacked down properly close to the ground; there's about 36 inches of air and skunks under the floor and the floor is not insulated with anything except tar-paper and dump rugs. The straw bales are fine to catch snow, but a little too porous to keep out the lurking frost. Snow is lovely insulation; besides being an agreeable color with blue hues on bright days, it is full of bitsy pockets of air that trap heat and keep the cold away from my reading chair and the cat's favorite lap. But it has not come yet and I pace with trepidation, the little stove hopping with twice the wood-load it would carry were we nested in and protected.

It's not serious yet, of course, just standard pre-winter neurosis. The nights this week have been hovering around zero—which is still shirt-sleeve weather to those who have been up here long enough to have blood as thick as homemade ketchup. No big deal. Two blankets, one cat-warmer against the chest, four logs burning lazy in the dark; we can handle it.

But I hate waiting. You know you're ready, but the longer you wait the more little devils come into the brain and you find yourself futzing the days away, doing things that might-maybe need doing. I hate futzing also.

One winter, during the drought years, the snow didn't come until late—near the first of the year, in fact—but the temperatures got down into the -50° and -60° range, which the little cabin doesn't handle well without its outer blanket of protection. The cat and I would sit near the stove and watch the frost capture the door-knob, then the edges of the door and windowsills turned white, then the icy fingers would begin to creep out across the carpet from under the door and the zillion gaps in the places where the floor meets the walls. It was like a B-Movie: *The Frost Comes.* The cat would look at me and I would stuff the other half of the Targhee Forest in the little stove, and still the frost would come.

That year during one of the extended cold spells, we brought the skunks in, set out an incubation heat-lamp for the chickadees on the porch, and built a platform of books and manuscripts (to get up off the floor) near the stove, covered it with wool blankets, brought in about a half-cabin of split wood, and rode out the cold on our little island in the center of the one-room. The skunks were polite, the cat aloof, and I was fine: I could reach the now-inside woodpile without having to take down the barricade of laundry guarding the gaps in the door and could reach under the blankets for reading matter. I would read out loud—Byron, Plutarch, Fu Manchu stories, whatever—to the furry ones, and loud enough for the birds (about forty of them) on the porch to hear, huddled under their lamp with a mountain of unfrozen black sunflower seeds nearby.

The cold broke after five days and the carpet was wet for a week from the melted frost. I waited until I was sure it was at least two sunny degrees outside, evicted the skunks, and went out and cranked up the saw to replace the forlorn-looking woodpile. We had burned a little over two cords of wood in five days, just to heat a 14x16 room, but we did fine, even the mice in the walls rode it out with dignity.

That was late November, if I remember right. It was interesting and challenging, as mountain life should be, even amusing. But it was a funny-once type of experience and I have come to appreciate early snow years as being very handy.

So I am ready and waiting, but she hasn't come yet, and you can only prepare so much for the guest in white that is never the same from each year to the next.

THE WHITE LADY

The funny man sits in the little cabin in front of the medium stove, packed with wood, and wears wool socks, running shorts, and a Soviet-style muskrat hat, flaps down, the fur on the cap merging and folding into the beard on his face. The cat is amused, but is also in the lap where the thermals are just right, and purrs with symbiotic warmth, letting the funny man know that he, the cat, has known him a long time and understands the situation.

Which is this: as I write, the snow has not come. Even Sawtelle, just a few inches short of 10,000 feet high, has only a little grey in its beard. Lesser Frogpond, my home, is suspended like a ramshackle birdhouse on cinder block piers about three feet in the air. The air is cold. There is no snow to block the air when it takes notions to move around and move in. Drafty is not the right word for the little hut; it seems to invite the north wind right on in, where it swirls around looking for warm-blooded prey.

So the hovel gets divided up into three distinct, horizontal thermal zones. The floor is below freezing, Father Frost having set up shop under the boards and busily making cold-toes devices, shaping the wind into packets of chill and hanging them under my feet—hence the wool socks. From about the knees to the neck (measured on a six-foot standing hermit), the temperature is about 85°, the stove hopping mad with too much wood and making freight train noises in the pipe, trying to do its job, but it's like trying to heat an old tin can that's been shot full of too many holes, more than drafty, so it can only hold a straight-ahead, at the belly, kind of heat—hence the running shorts. From the chin up, the north wind plays inside, like so many bats in a gothic belfry, flapping about noisily, and you have to duck to avoid the drafts.

From outside, in the dark, you can see light leaking out from under the eaves where the squirrels have stolen all the insulation for their own nests. The sight from outside would be pretty for a lantern or postcard, but puts the trembles to the hovel-owner who has to winter there—hence the fur cap. Besides, my grandmother told me if my feet were cold to put on a hat, so I am covering my bets as best I can. The little shack has its own interior weather systems, just as a wildfire creates its own wind-storms, and snow would stop all this nonsense and steady down the thermal layers into one nice little box of heat. But the snows have not come, and so the cat and I must wait patiently, me in my costume and he in my lap, for the comfort of being nestled in the white lady's arms.

Meanwhile the cat has become strange, I think. I say 'I think', because he has odd ways that take some years to see the logic to, and I am not a proper judge of odd ways, having a fine repertoire of them myself. But of late, he has taken to bringing in guests from the cold. (As if the frost below and the blizzard in the rafters did not make for a full house already.) He is a good cat, possessed of kindness and no little compassion, but I am suspicious since the guests he prances in with are all white-footed deer mice.

He brings them in held snugly under his whiskers, the little bodies in that possum-like shock he can induce, but otherwise uninjured. He doesn't try to sneak them in (the cabin is tilted slightly forward, by design, so that he may open and close the door himself); he comes in full of purpose, looks around for awhile, and releases the mice here and there, then goes out for more, the little bodies coming to life once he is back outside and fading with scurry into the shadows and corners. I am amused, and too cold to do anything about it, curled into a fetal position with a book in the middle thermal zone.

The mice soon find that zone, and the other night I noticed the 'j' on the old typewriter was sticking, so I punched it a little harder and got a startled squeek as a mouse dashed out from beneath. I lifted the machine and found a fine little nest under the keyboard. I now check the blankets before going to bed at night.

Perhaps I am underestimating (again) the old cat. He is a thoughtful type, and I have finally decided he is doing a version of getting in the wood. Without snow, the mice would retreat deep into the woods and burrows and be inconvenient to fetch for a winter snack. So I think he is stocking the pantry, hoarding up a series of warm meals on the hoof that he won't be required to go out in the cold and toil after. It is a sign of a very long winter or a very smart cat, I am not sure which.

But I sure wish it would snow.

1994

THE END OF THE RAINBOW

The in-keeping, enfolding time of the year has come to our mountains. The major festivals of harvest and renewal have passed and the high valleys have pulled up the blanket, snuffed the candle, let out a long chill breath, and gone to bed. In Island Park there is a fine blanket of snow, three feet and more up high, seed and soul slowed under the vast meadow of white calm. No big storms yet this winter-year, though they will surely come, two or twenty, it does not matter, they will all be welcomed home in their time. They belong here, the storms, as much as the winter constellations that come howling brightly up out of the east; Orion, the hunter, and the Pleiades, my birth stars, chasing the full moon of this week across the sky. Like many others, I came to this Last Best Place from somewhere else (I did not even see snow fall from the sky until I was 17 years old) and was captured by the grace of feeling sensible and proportionately small; it felt like home and I was a pilgrim no more. The storms taught me things and challenged my self-importance, the long winter nights taught me to think slowly and carefully and accept my minor role as caretaker and guest of these mountains and my life, to ponder in the long dark and play the day with the wonder of a small child.

I home on a good half-acre at the end of an old road that sneaks off through the trees like an evening deer, off of an even older quiet road, near but not on the river, the Henrys Fork, the splendid main artery of the old volcano. I can hear the swans and geese call to each other on the river during the long winter nights and they are a chorus to the stars, a lullaby heard sharply across the snow. There are aspen and pine in the yard, none grand but all eloquent, and one first spring, years ago, I heard a brief choir of frogs in the swale below the one-room cabin and, in a fit of the cutes, named the place

Lesser Frogpond. It was a suitable and proper name for the home of one who has my habits and vocation, and my companion, an old tom cat named P'o, was well-pleased enough with the quiet and the fur-only neighbors, so we nested up in front of the small stove that first winter and have never found reason to leave since. It is home.

Winter has become a busy place these last few years in Island Park. Where once we all rolled over into another time zone and pace in winter, living like squirrels off the cache from summer's hasty season, now we have become a major regional playground and destination. That has disturbed the quiet a little and made the few roads more fraught with hazard and traffic, but the grand beauty remains; large enough to accept the storms and visitors, full enough to pass the cup with all. As a practicing hermit, I should have first rights on the complaint to shut the gate after I got here, but I do not feel so. This place, my home, is a gift, a feast to be shared.

I became 46 years old last year and the best, the most bountiful and grateful years, have been these last, these seasons in the mountains. I wish for the visitors to have what we who live here have: a chance to locate themselves, balance themselves, on a stage so grand that they become lost in wonder and found in spirit. All are welcome; we have found the end of the rainbow here—no gold, but heart-felt laughter around a good fire and simple joy. It is a large cup. There is a certain responsibility to share with others, make easily available to others, this treasure we who live here have daily. I do not wonder that they want to come here; I did. I have not spent my years here, I bought them at the happy price of choosing to live in modest circumstances surrounded by sumptious quality. It has been a bargain and a constant education. I know that many of the visitors would like to stay here, perhaps even to live here, for I see the hunger in their eyes that was in mine when I first came across the edge of the caldera. Most, of course, cannot stay. Many have obligation to others in other places, some cannot accept the storms and the long winter nights, a few cannot tolerate the rapture.

I love this high valley and take it very personally, but I do not think it should be a secret or a private sanctuary. There is too much bounty here to be hoarded by a few. Even those who come and must leave can take away with them as much of the end of the rainbow as their heart dare carry. And they can come back. They are welcome back.

Like the storms, I would be surprised not to see them wish to come back. Welcome, all.

FACING THE LIGHT

Amoment of morning can change the day. Last week the sky emptied a foot-fall of new storm and then broke up into sunshine, the fresh snow as soft and heavy as a swan's breast, the light captured and magnified in the meadows then thrown back into the thin chill air, glimmering the forest, delighting the eye. The days are beginning to fill out now all over this upper half of the planet, but in Island Park, where the land is high edges and narrow hollows, the shortening of the shadows is more noticible, more pungent, more promising. In most Other Places, it will be mid-February before the shadow of winter is seen to depart, but up here, out near the edge of the world, the old man has already turned his back to the light.

After the storm, the dawn. I sat by the river, cradled in a nest of young firs, and watched the stars wink out as the mountain turned to face the light. Winter mornings are a special canvas, primed with translucent cold, color and detail suspended and frozen until released by the touch of rosy-fingered dawn. All things are extreme in winter in the high mountains; extreme temperatures, extreme discomfort for the unwary, extreme beauty and joy for the watchful and inspired. The winter canvas has sharply-defined edges between the pictured subjects, the Painter's brush forcing things together in the unmoving cold, mixing the pallet with sharp light; no soft melding of summer's pastels here, in an often-wasted word: things are different.

I folded my arms around my knees, drawn up into a huddle in the cold, watching—waiting—out over the river, as the east pushed at the dark. She joined me then, there for the moment. The sun bloomed. The morning beckoned and fetched away the night.

Like a golden laser, beams reached out between the silent and standing trees and touched the river. In the path of light, a mist rose slowly from the water, but only in those places touched by the light; the dark channels of water between remained in night. In fact, the sunlight is a laser, condensing and making visible the moisture suspended in the frozen air. The rising mist came from the atmosphere encountering the radiation of morning beams, and not from the river itself. The Painter stirred the pallet. I pulled a hand from my coat and gestured out over the river, not speaking. She nodded, not looking at me, not needing to say anything.

The morning rose abundant and rebounded off the back of the clouds of the retreating storm, filling the river with gold, color and form coming brightly to the canvas. Music joined the moment, and the swans drifted into the corridors of morning on the river and rejoiced. The little ones, chickadees and red squirrels, shook free of the cold and emerged at the edges of branches, announcing the day. It was wonderful. It was another day in the Rockies and it was wonderful.

She turned to me and smiled, her breath and words shaping lightly in the sunshine, like the graceful mist over the water. She said: I think perhaps I know why we have met in this place. I watched— waited on her words gaily. She said: a painter loves those who love his work, appreciates those who appreciate the craft and excellence, wants them to be together to share the exhibition of his art. She flipped a wrist artfully at the river and morning and sunshine and birdsong. She said: this is a special moment and we see it so and the Painter has brought us well-met together to enjoy His work.

She talks like that. Really. It is a constant refreshment to hear her speak that way about these things and is one of the many reasons I adore her company. She rose from the bank of the river in one lovely motion and went her way. I looked out over the canvas and knew the rest of the day would be a constant morning in the Rockies.

Wonderful.

THE CARETAKERS

Mid-winter can nip at your attitude if you do not pay attention well and often. I awoke at my estate of Lesser Frogpond one morning last week, pulled back the rag curtains of the one-room hovel, and looked out on a landscape that mirrored the color of my mind: grey. I pulled at my mid-winter beard, also grey. I reached for the coffee cup last washed when the opsrey remained; it was also grey. Island Park is up in the rafters of the world, shoulder to shoulder with the clouds, and sometimes those clouds move right in on top of you, riding January into the blues. There is no January thaw in Island Park, it comes in February, limping. There is no spring in April, it comes for fifteen minutes of May. It is a gadzillion weeks until May. I put down the curtains, put down the coffee cup, and took back to my bed.

Your grandmother had one of those small globes on a stand with a winter scene within—a cottage or reindeer or some such— that you inverted with both child-hands and then turned back over to watch the snow fall inside. I have one of those globes on the stump beside my bed. It is there in July to remind the mosquitoes of their fate, it is there in January to remind me that I am not inside looking out. I turned the globe—it now fits comfortably in one weathered hand—but it did not work properly that grey morning. We've had some snow this week and the coming and going of things is tricky. I cannot be snowed in because there are skis and snowshoes on the porch, and I am a fellow who abides his own company well. But I can be snowed out, removed by my own mood from the luster of my own home and luxury of winter's silence. I put the little device back on the stump and growled softly at the old cat. He ignored January and me, his tail twitching softly in sleep as he chased June's butterflies in his dreams.

Fortunately I have help. The winter caretakers of my lands are merry pranksters and impudent to the baron when he is too full of himself and snowed out. I stepped out onto the porch for some stovewood and was mobbed by the chickadees, my caretakers. The mountain chickadee is the one with the racy stripe of pearl-white running along and beside its eye. During the drought years some of the valley black-capped chickadees (no eye stripe) snuck up the hill, but real winter returned last year and chased them off, leaving the mountain chickadees to their rightful domain. They are the toughest thing alive; tougher than me, tougher than winter, all heart and guts and wry humor. I have watched them on a morning of 60 below in the pale pine outside my window, encased in ice, still as stones, surely frozen into finality. The dawn would strike them, they would give a shake out of their cocoon, bark a little at the cold, then tumble onto the porch looking for the peanut butter that is part of the price of their company. If there is none, and there was none this morning, they lay in wait for me to emerge and then pester me into action. And laughter, always.

They do not fly like a bird, they fly like an acrobat on swings of breeze and sunbeams. They caw and bray and honk and sometimes even chirp. They pull at my hair and sleeve and rocket between my legs and tickle my fancy. On mornings when I am too snowed out and cannot emerge beyond door or self, they line the windowsill and peck at the glass reminding me of the chores and the duty of a life come wished-full. One winter morning when I was very ill, they sat like sentinels quietly, watching over me, caretaking. This morning they cracked my surliness with their clowning. I shook off my cocoon and went inside to fetch treats, glopped more coffee into the cup and went back out to commune. I pulled up a log and leaned against the woodpile while they encircled the porch and me, the charm bracelet of winter, all feathers and flash. It is a fine thing to be snowed in with friends. We gossiped and argued as the sun burned off the mist and the grey blossomed golden.

I looked up and she was standing in the yard, the snow up to her gentle waist. I never hear her coming, never know of her coming, always a surprise, always welcome. She tossed a lock of hair out of her eyes, hair like dark feathers on her cheek. I shook a chickadee out of my beard and grinned out at her. The corners of her mouth turned cupid-up, an endearing sign of mischief below the enduring mystery of her eyes.

The birds come to you, she said.

No, I said, I come to them.

Good morning, I said.

Yes, she said.

ASSUMPTION OF RISK

The other night, jawing in front of the stove, a lawyer friend brought up the concept of "assumption of the risk." It's legal term that means (loosely) that if you see a sign that says: Don't Go Out To The Edge, and you go out to the edge and fall out into the nothing, the edge is not liable for your fall; you were warned. A kind of "I Know What I'm Doing" clause in the contract you've made with some parts of your life. Later on I got to thinking it over and the whole idea made my brain itch. Are we each and ourselves responsible for our own actions? Yes. Always. I have seen it often and it is so. Do accidents happen? Yes, sorry. Just as part of the contract with life is death, so are accidents and surprises and the befallen unexpected part of the fabric in the pattern. Are we responsible for the unexpected? I don't know. I'm not even sure I care; you are there and participate, and that is enough. If that frightens you—and it should—don't go near the edge.

It grew colder last week in Island Park. Even with blanketing snow, the frost reaches under and into the edges of things and you feel the crisp more keenly. The night sky is flagrant with stars, the winter constellations rising earnestly each night. Each evening as I go out for another armload of wood, the moon grows bolder, waxing to full on the nights of last week. Winter, another winter, has climbed the mountains, and I sit closer to the fire and wonder over the assumption of risk.

Island Park is my favorite place in the world. It will steal your heart off, leaving you completely devoted, and it will try and kill you some fine days; sometimes with ironic beauty and sometimes with blizzards or bears. You can get very cold here, or very isolated, or fall in love, or get snowed in and over here; it is risky place.

So why assume the risk when there are options and other places less close to the edge? Respect. I respect this place, Island Park, my home. I am honored to live here, it commands my attention, demands my best efforts, and I am awed at the magic that can happen in such a place. After all these years I have lost the need to prove anything against the weather or the wild things, and am left with a simple pleasure: I'm having fun.

You have nothing left to prove? she asked with the devil in her eyes that are the color of grouse wings. I have ambitions, I have dreams, I said, but I know what I'm doing and I'm willing to fail for the sheer joy of the trying of it. No, nothing to prove, I said. I will take the challenges and respect the accidents. It is a good life, I said.

I would like to move here, to Island Park, she said, to so near the edge and near you. I looked away, embarrassed with joy. The snows have come, I said, and it will be difficult and inconvenient until May, the cold will make things tighten and constrict your life. It is an in-keeping time that you must be sure of to endure, to assume the risk.

Is it possible? she said. I looked out the window at an army of stars. Yes, I said, there is a cabin I can borrow, a snug cabin enough miles from here, from Lesser Frogpond and from me. Yes, it can be done, if that is what you wish.

She looked out the window at a vortex of stars, this woman who had become less of a stranger and more than a friend, an accident of the mountains, an accident of unlooked for magic. She is beautiful and bright, I thought, and bold and scared. I respect her honesty, with herself and with me and with these mountains, and she would do well in this place.

I would leave too much behind, perhaps, she said. Bring what you can and cherish and visit the rest, I said. I will have to consider, to go away and consider, she said and talk with many, many people. Yes, I said. I must be sure, she said. Yes, I said, you must be sure or you will not be able to assume the risk and it will break your heart.

She stood with her hand on the door, ready to go back down and away. She turned and smiled in the shallow light and said: what would the most dangerous thing here be, the most risk, the greatest thing to frighten me?

I looked out the window at a heaven of stars.

That I love you, I said, and you might become lost in the storm of that.

She smiled more and caught all the light of the small room in her eyes. Or found, she said, and stepped lightly out under the waiting stars.

MARCH WINDS

The March wind is a foul companion. It howled like a banshee under the eaves during the nights of last week's dark moon. The wind came with its imps and familiars, red-wing blackbirds, who set up a gluttony at the feeding station and a cacophony of cackles and shrieks during the daylight. It rose out of the south like a hot-blooded army and tore at the snowpack, teasing the aspen to bud, and stirring the unwary birds to begin their yearly pairing dances.

It is too early. Go away. It is not time. Taking the snow in March is like ripping the covers from a sleeper when the resting has not been completed and the threat of cold has not gone away. There will be below-zero nights well into April and the buds will freeze and the young birds will die. It is an ill wind and will bear no good if it does not depart soon.

Island Park is a protected valley, a Shangri-La of sorts, and except for up near Henry's Lake, we are not used to wind and it makes us uneasy. The wind in March whispers and taunts when we are all weak with winter and dreamy and gullible. For the idle, it is a temptation to wish for a short-cut around the season, a discount to the price paid for making a home so high against the weather. It is heard that Ennis, to the north in Montana, is green. Ashton, just a few miles and a thousand feet down to the south, has always had four weeks less winter than us, two less weeks on each end. The heart begins to yearn. Longing pecks at the seed and sap saying: get up and begin. It is another and a pest, this wind in March.

One morning early while, the crust was still crisp, I went out over the snow into the deep forest, away from the full siren-song of the wind. It was too warm—warm enough to take off my shirt and let the sun pick at my skin. I went looking for, and into, nests in the old lodgepoles and cavities of harboring aspen, looking for those who might have been betrayed by the sly-soft, early wind. Before the sun had grown higher than the highest trees, I picked up the faint trail of the coyote and soon, the coyote himself. He was doing the same as myself, looking over nest sites, but as a predator, not a pilgrim. He was gaunt and furtive, but we know each other, so when he had caught my eye with his, he continued his search and I mine.

A few weeks ago there were two sets of tracks, and I wondered if his mate had taken to the den, for it is their proper time, or if she had fallen to the rising price of pelt. We meandered into a meadow in the forest, a low opening where there would be a vernal pond before the late summer baked it to mud and dry reeds. It is one of those places beloved by wildlife, with food in the clearing and cover at the edges. The coyote took one edge and I took the other, our tracks wandering through the willows and dead trees. Not many had been fooled by the wind and most nests were empty and waiting. I reached into one hole, stretching on the skis with my arm beyond my head, and heard the sharp chirp of a flying squirrel who emerged enraged and flattened on the aspen trunk, chattering me off. It is their proper time also, and I let it be.

Across the meadow I heard the coyote snuffling among the willows. The wind had disturbed the scents and confused the sounds he hunts by, but something had brought him alert. He started digging in the snow and a ragged hoof showed, the beginning of a winter-killed deer and a carrion meal. He yelped and whistled, digging faster. The tree over him blossomed ravens and a magpie floated in through the pines. I smiled at the gathering crowd; in a hungry time, the neighbors would eat this day.

That night I lay buried in a book and listened to the tin rattle in the wind on the cabin roof. The stove smoked and slumbered. In the late hours the cat came and curled against my leg and I also noticed the chill, getting up to fetch a log. Outside a single owl began to sing softly. I stepped out on the porch to gather the sound. The wind had died and the stars grown close and the cold returned, deepening and familiar. I put a few logs in my arm and felt with my nose out into the dark. Perhaps March would be fine. I went inside, petted the cat and went to bed.

GRACE

There are ducks in the puddles and a whisper of green rides on the wind. The osprey have returned to the nest above the cabin, and the season is getting as warm and frisky as a new puppy. There is still snow—there is always snow somewhere in Island Park—but it is a good melt, paced and flower-producing, a slow melt. Adagio. Timely.

Time is a grace, a friend monk once told me. We sat together in a spring like this one, in another place not like this one, and watched the snow melt slowly, the sun raising banners of green from the warming ground to proclaim victory. It had been a hard winter; perhaps he meant that "all comes to he who waits," perhaps he meant something more subtle and deep that I could not capture.

The mountains will calm the hurry out of you. With such a small part in such a large drama, you learn not to push the action. It can be pesky waiting for spring in this high valley, when all around and below you the plants are leafing out knee-high and the young birds are already tumbling down the breeze. Change has its own timetable here; you must participate daily to notice it, not merely observe and judge. You must track the snowbanks every day to find the trail of spring's changes.

"You wish change?" the fellow asked one day when I had complained about something not happening in accordance with my personal schedule. "Twelve thousand years ago the ice was here always, and now it is not. Four times a year the seasons change. If that is not soon enough, twice a day the whole world changes fundamentally—they are called tides. Is that soon enough for you?"

I had laughed at so direct an answer all those years ago. Simple enough, though perhaps more subtle than I will ever know. Pace yourself.

The marmots are out early this year, grazing like small brown sheep between the snowbanks. They are the last of our community to come out of hibernation and the first to go in, long before the snows.

They only spend a quarter of their lives awake and yet are astonishingly aware of the mood of the seasons, the curve of the moon, the place of the wind. I wonder if their dreams inform them, a metronome of images ticking away deep in the den.

I went to visit the bears a while back. They are well, grazing like large brown cows between the snowbanks, fueling the quick aware-ness that must release them from dormancy. Though not true hibernators, they must also pace themselves over a short year. They are social briefly in April—for the usual reasons—and then are off about the business of putting on weight and being surly until they den up during a major snowstorm in October or November; a major storm because the bears have adapted to being stalked to their lairs by early human hunters and wait for a heavy snowfall to cover their tracks. Pacing again.

One of spring's changes always arrives sooner than we wish, and to give parity this hibernator needs comment: the mosquitoes came calling last week, grazing on my arm. There is so much to look forward to, to gush over, about spring, that I always forget to include these pests in my longing for the season. Actually, like the poor, they are always with us, and I have seen a few hardy examples come buzzing by during an extended mid-winter thaw. Where they den up to be able to pester me in February I have no idea. The spring mosquitoes are the size of small hummingbirds and make a similar noise. Fortunately, the chill April nights make them torpid and dull, so they can be fetched away to another plane of existence without much effort or craft.

Last Saturday was a peach of a spring day in the mountains, the finest so far. I was resting idly on the porch in a puddle of sunlight, feeding the mosquitoes, when one of the neighbors dropped by, recently arrived from one of the other places.

"Survived another winter, I see, " he said.

"Dumb luck," I said, helping a mosquito off to another life. "I'm good at dumb luck."

We chatted up the morning, grazing the subjects of timing and the pace necessary to enjoy the adagio moments of spring life in Island Park.

"How do you make sure you're here at the right time for all this stuff?" he asked, after we'd watched the osprey dancing off beyond the porch and I'd pointed out the buttercups lying like new gold coins in the yard.

I leaned back in the new sunlight and smiled. "I never leave".

ROOM WITH A VIEW

The Annual Quack this year is about crowds—how things are getting dense and clustered up here in Shangri-La. Boy howdy, I agree. Why, just the other morning down at my estate at Lesser Frogpond there was a crowd control crisis. First I had to elbow the old cat, the house skunk, and various ground squirrels (who had come inside for breakfast) out of the way to get me and my coffee forth to the door. Then I was marauded by a herd of birds on the porch who were in a rage about the ground squirrels eating all their seed and peanut butter. I shoveled fodder onto one stump and sat upon the other for my morning meditations. Out on the river a pair of young moose grazed the watercress and lillies. Down in the swale four deer nibbled at the new-bright weeds and swayed in the morning sunshine. The osprey sailed over with a fistful of fresh fish to feed the mate tending eggs. A salmonfly fell in my coffee cup and several more nested in my hair. The mosquitoes stood in line for my body.

I got up and proceeded around the corner to the outbuilding with the crescent moon for further meditations, nodding a good morning to the bison that was standing in front of my truck. I stopped and looked him over; the old bulls wander out of the Park once in awhile and frump around our valley for a few months before heading back. It's getting damn crowded here, I thought, but the bison was a big old boy—about eye-level with my six feet—and I decided not to press the issue. These old bulls are no more social than I am and require no entertaining or tea, so I let him mow the dandelions and went on. He could join the rest of the morning crowd on the porch for all I cared.

Crowded? Compared to what? If you think it is crowded in Island Park, where have you come from? I've been in the most populated cities in the world and I know a crowd from a glee club and I moved here to join the glee club. Certainly there are more people than when I came here, but they have come for the same reasons I did and that is fine with me. This place healed and grew me and I hope it does the same for them. Certainly there are more people coming to buy homes here; I did, and I wish them well and welcome them. Certainly the highway is getting thick; so did the pioneer trails of the last century when folks headed out for a better land. They're doing it now and good for them.

Kindly read my printed lips: Less than 11% of Island Park is private land. Much of that land is patchworked over the valley because many of the homesteads were patented-up in the 1890's and the National Forest had to build its turf around them when it came into being in 1907. I can step out my door and be in a forest we all own in less than three minutes, on foot, with a game knee. Almost anyone living in Island Park can do the same.

Island Park is very much one of the Last Best Places. I have whimpery, petty moments when I come across some pilgrim standing next to one of my personal fish in the river, or picnicing in a forest glade I considered my own secret, but I have never seriously thought about closing the gate after I got here. There are simply too many fish, too many great spots, to get greedy over. Some of them may require a little hike, a small lurching forth from the convenient traveling womb of the truck, but that does not seem so much to ask. In 1993, with a gadzillon visitors, it was documented in Yellowstone Park that less than 2% of those visitors ever went farther than a quarter of a mile from their vehicle. Too bad. Like Island Park, Yellowstone has plenty of uncrowded places just off the road. Plenty of room, with a view.

Some, due to age or infirmity, cannot hike. Years ago a friend arrived who had been injured in the war. There is a spot in south Harriman Park where an eagle's nest spires out over a bubbly spring creek. It is not far by foot, if you know the way. The nest and the spring will make you believe in Grace and smile a lot. I pushed his chair down the trail where I could and carried him where the chair wouldn't go. It was not far and it was worth it; for him and for me.

Noblesse Oblige, my friends and neighbors, we all need to help each other out here. We who are privilged to live here need to make the small effort to share the wealth, to help those who wish a piece of the dream. We are all guests in a sense, all members of the glee club.

GOOD CATCH

A friend came by over the weekend seeking fish, sanity, and a lack of species-congestion. I'm in love with his wife and kids and so is he, so we get along fine, and I took him forth to the Secret Spot, family in tow. We stood on the bank and I held out an arm.

"See that rock near the far bank? George the Third lives two cubits south of the rock in that riffle on this side."

"George III?" said my friend.

"Yeh, spelled like that too," I said. "I named him after the British king during the Revolutionary War because he's fat and slothful and very crazy. Now to get there you have to cross the river from here and wade that shallow stretch of slippery boulders. See it? It's the spot where the sign says 'There be Crocodiles Here'. Then there's a deep channel just this side of the rock where the sign says 'Feets Don't Fail Me Now'. You stand on this side of the channel and fetch George."

The friend looked me over. He's never been quite sure of my intentions.

"You say this fish is crazy?" he said.

"You bet," I said. He seldom ever rises, just lays there thinking deep thoughts and fooling around in the current."

"So how do I fetch him," said the friend smiling.

"We could chum the water with the children," I said looking over my shoulder at the brood.

"Three of the children are over six feet tall," he said.

"It's a big fish," I said. "Actually, he likes to be caught. Here. Take this big old Elk Hair Caddis that's been run over by the carpet sweeper a few times and chewed up by the cat. George likes this fly. Honest."

I gave the friend the mashed up piece of debris and he strapped it on the front of his line and stepped out into the river. He's a good man and I am fond of him, and George is a fine fish and I owe them both, so I thought the game well-met.

The day blazed and the children spread out in the water and the osprey swept a few feet over their heads, protecting his turf, and I sat on the bank and chatted up the wife. This is a good thing, I thought. They are the kind of company I like to keep. Bright healthy people with a love for the mountains and the rivers that flow here. They become the place and the place becomes them.

He stood on the edge of the channel and shook off a few of the smaller, foot-and-a-half fish that were drawn to the magic fly. He looked across the river at me and I nodded and smiled.

George came up like one of those German U-Boats surfacing in a war movie, bit down hard on the fly, rolled into the channel and darned near pulled my friend in along with him. My friend's back arched in surprise and he pulled the rod tip up while dancing on the rocks under the surface. The rod bent and the line sang and the sun shown. George lay on the bottom waiting for my friend to get a grip and then swooshed across the river. My friend planted the rod-butt at belt line and hung on, like a sport fisherman chained to a marlin.

About mid-stream, George jumped out and the children stopped and stared. It was like a watching a dirigible, fins and all, break the surface. We could hear the splash from our bank when he dove back in the water. Cheers and whoops went up and, after a seemly time, my friend netted George, unhooked him, patted him like a big dog, and pushed him back into the channel. It was a wonderful thing, a finer moment.

We sat in the evening watching the river flow. "He does like to be caught," my friend said, "but I liked it even more letting him go."

We sat in the evening watching his wife sit brightly on the bank playing with rose blossoms and stoneflies. "But she is a keeper," he said.

"That she is," I said. "Keep her well, please." I held out my hand. "But I'll take my old fly back. You will all return more often that way."

He laughed and handed it over, and across the river the fish pondered.

GETTING INDEPENDENT

A good guru should be temporary. A good teacher should position you, line you up to attempt your goal, and then get out of the way while you kick the thing.

One evening many years ago I was sitting with a friend of mine—a small man of large heart—when he held a hand out to the dark. I looked at his hand, and he wrinkled his brow and shook his head. I looked out into the dark where his hand was pointing and saw the moon rising over the western mountains, and he smiled and nodded. Never confuse the pointing with the moon, he said, or the messenger with the message. He rose quietly and left me alone with the glowing moon. Perhaps nothing is so exciting or frightening as a departing guru.

So it was when the porcupine left. You understand that it can be risky business to keep a porcupine; you can become attached to the beast—or parts of it—the same way you can become attached to other things in life, gurus and their guidance, for instance.

This porcupine happened upon me one fine July Fourth weekend, when I was hiding out beside a small stream in a far spot of our valley. I am a bleeding-heart conservative and a patriot, I suppose, but I don't consider the need to celebrate our nation as a team sport unless we are at war or the food is free. I was watching a fine fish rise when something bumped gently into my back. I peered around and saw the porcupine shuffling off. After a few moments it bumped into a stump and started to climb, but the snag was only two feet tall and it stopped and began to chirp softly. I went over and stood by the animal; it was a small porcupine, more tired than afraid, I thought, and it whistled at me but did not threaten. You can stroke a porcupine with the grain (a subject for another column, but I'll let it be for now) and I smoothed the quills back from its face and bent down and saw that its eyes were cloudy-white. The animal was stone blind. I sighed and picked up the porcupine (with the grain) and we went home.

Back in the cabin, porcupine in my lap, the old cat looked at the animal and looked at me and sighed. I had fetched down from the loft a diluted solution of boric acid that I kept among the necessaries. Rabbits sometimes get an infection of the eyes, I have forgotten the name, that clouds the surface of the lens like a milky cataract. It can be treated with regular bathing of boric acid solution; I had successfully healed a muskrat of the affliction that way one spring. I daubed the juice on, which is painless, and set the animal down on the floor. It ran the walls until it found the screen door and I went over and let it out. I don't cage things, even things that might need caging. I've been caged by one thing and another before and won't abide doing it in my personal life anymore. It bumped around the porch, knocking over some things, chirped for awhile in frustration, and then seemed to catch my scent where I was standing in the door watching and came and stood by my leg until I bent down and fetched it, and we went in for the evening.

I found it would eat peanut butter and carrots. I had plenty, so I didn't have to bring in a tree. It took a corner of the cabin and settled and seemed content. The cat and I were careful where we stepped in the dark and we all got along. After a week of treatment, its vision seemed to clear some, and I think it could see a little light, for it took to standing at the door when the morning was on the porch, but showed no signs of being well enough to want to leave. I had become fond of the porcupine. It abided my ways and we took to talking—me mostly—about things that come and go.

The best thing, I said to the porcupine, is to just love her, to want good to happen for her, her life to be full, full of her own lights.

I sponged some more solution on its eyes. It blinked, but never moved, the quills alert, the nose listening.

The next best thing would be to be in love with her, you know, holding hands out in the pines and sharing the fire come evening and such. The porcupine whistled, and I moved to the other eye.

I'm very lucky, I said, I really am, to have the best thing, the honorable thing. She is doing very well on her own, independent. I can't really regret not having the rest, now can I?

One morning I awoke and the porcupine was sitting near my head and its eyes were clear and bright. I arose and went and opened the door, the porcupine shuffling along behind me. It went out and stopped on the porch and looked up at me; looked up very well. I nodded and smiled and it switched its tail and went down the steps and out into the forest.

I see the porcupine once in a while when I am deep in the trees. It chirps but we do not approach each other closely as that would not be proper. It was a good guru, and I am proud of the porcupine for being well and staying that way. Its picture is on my wall along with other teachers that have departed from me.

THE MOOSE

I was torpiding around in the afternoon heat hating the flies that pranced in the sunbeams. The highway has finally gotten to me. I am putting in too many miles with too many people; a little over 2000 miles a month on two-lane roads with four-lane drivers, thousands of them. My worst nightmare is to be driving the asphalt arteries of Los Angeles. I shivered in the heat and snarled at one of the gadzillion house chipmunks. I decided all the traffic was chasing off the wildlife and making a nervous wreck—to coin a phrase—of my pastoral life.

It used to be merely a mess from Memorial Day to Labor Day, a few weeks in the months of Paradise. Now it is always. I mourn the winter runs to the press at 26 miles an hour on black ice, the freedom and safety of the open road, the brief respites in the whiteouts letting you get your bearings while not being worried about the other guy in your lane. The other guy was thirty miles away and going slow also. No more. It's a speedway of folks in a hurry to have fun, summer and winter. There isn't enough room on the two lanes for us all and it scares me, makes me leave fingerprints on the steering wheel of the old truck. I come back from the road and stoop to kiss the step on the porch and wonder why I should continue to live in a place that is festering with machines.

I stepped out at twilight and there was a moose in the yard roughly the size of Nebraska. We looked each other over, primitive recognizing primitive. I thought about the camera-machine but it was in the truck-machine and the moose was between me and them. Moose are the most prehistoric-looking of our neighbors and I imagine it was thinking of men who looked a lot like me, rattling thick spears over smoky fires and praying for a treasure of meat a lot like him.

A car came halfway up the dead-end road and broke the spell for both us. The moose muttered off into the aspen at the edge of the cabin, and I went over and looked at his track. There are moose and there are moose; three subspecies of *Alces alces* (Deer deer) in our area and none before the mid-1880's. Our local subspecies is the smallest of the group, but this one was no puppy. The car decided it was lost, or ought to be, and left, turning on its lights in the lowering dusk. A thin moon nested at the top of the aspen and I heard him begin go away down the swale. I moved next to a low fir and watched the bats begin to dance. A summer dog barked a little ways off and the moose came back up the swale and kept coming until he was also next to the low fir. I could have reached out and patted his nose. I did not. He snuffled me over and backed up a dozen feet to stand next to the outhouse. The top of his rack was even with the top of the outhouse. The top of the outhouse is eight feet tall.

The dog barked and the traffic moaned out on the distant highway. He looked around and then bent very far down and started grazing on the clover and yarrow. I sat down against the tree and said: we are both trapped here, you and me, backed up against the mountains. There is no other place for us, no better place, no place where we can live well and they cannot find us. The mountain shrugged off the heat with a breeze and the aspens rippled. But here there are moments like this, I said, where the moon is close and they are distant. More soft, round moments here at the end of a dusty road in the forest than any other place I have known or can imagine. This will have to do for now, I said, this is more than enough for now. You are safe this evening and so am I.

I went in and got an apple and went back out under the tree and rolled it to him. He fielded it well for all his bulk; I could hear him close his teeth wetly on it, his shadow a huge shape against the last glow of the western sky. The bats passed before the moon like moths in front of a lamp. I think he no longer saw a narrow-eyed hunter hulking in the dark; just another large mammal looking for a quiet corner of the evening. Hours later, midnight to judge by the turning of the Big Dipper in the north, I bid him well and went to bed. The next morning the moose was gone but he will be back and so will I. There are so few places and moments left to us.

TRANSPORT

Maybe I'm not male enough. It took me awhile to get with the program, much less understand it. A female friend of mine calls events like the situation with the truck a 'male thing', a phrase that irritates me beyond reason or understanding. Maybe I understand now.

Females should stop reading this, since you all seem to know these things about us anyway, and waxing bellicose in front of you will embarrass me and my half of the species.

I have acquired a 1962 Willys Jeep truck. It is fine transport and the rest of my aged fleet needed a rest. I liked the truck because it was within my limited price range. I liked it because it squatted next to the ground, some tons of steel and iron, and looked like it might stay there, instead of off the ice and into the ditch. I liked it because it had the original 1962 owner's manual in the glove box and someone had cared enough to keep it there. But I liked it most because it had lived in Island Park all its life; the original owner was the step-father of a friend of mine and, so the story goes, the truck was a poaching wagon in the late '60's in Island Park. Apparently the fellows would smell a few snowflakes and get whiskied up and head up the hills to make meat in the truck, hooves and boots hanging out everywhere. They'd four-wheel drive out past the law until the winter meat was in and have a grand old time. I don't poach, but my own history is not untarnished so I felt a fine kinship to the jeep, and took it home. That's when the situation began to happen.

I am not a mechanic. I did not know what or where a carburator was until I was 26 or 27 years old. The old jeep had been parked for quite a while on a side road, but nice things had been done to it.

The paint job is original but much of the rest is new or has been re-newed. I noticed when you stepped on the gas you got pressed back in the seat some, but the speedometer didn't work and I didn't think much about it. The engine also sounded a little like the deep purr of a saber-toothed tiger, and I thought that was nice.

I pulled up to the office and a red-blooded male American Republican came over and drooled on the tire. I turned the tiger off.

"Shoot Golly!" he said. "Whatchoo got there?"

"Something wrong?" I asked.

He lifted the hood and looked down like he'd just found a new copy of the Sports Illustrated Swimsuit Edition. He cussed in manly and sweet ways. He walked around the truck looking upon and under things.

"Whatchoo got here," he said, "is a solid steel vehicle with a PTO zillion-pound winch hanging on the front and new 16 inch wheels on 11 inch new brakes and new hubs and," his eyes began to shine, "a 283 V8 Chevy engine with twin pipes."

"Is that good?" I said.

He pulled his belt buckle up over his stomach and grinned east and west. "That's just dandy," he said.

I got with the program. I got out and pulled up my belt buckle over my stomach and waved at the inside. "It's got red carpet," I said.

"Bright as a pagan whorehouse," he said. He shifted to a serious, man-to-man squint. "How much money you need to have for that?"

I'm no rube, so I translated that he wanted to buy it. I squinted back sorrowfully and got in and stepped on the tiger, shaking my head. He nodded perfect, male-bonding, understanding and I left him in the dust.

The situation keeps happening. The entire male population of Livingston, Montana came to the curbs and stared when I went to press that week. Elderly farmers got tears in their eyes when I would drive buy. I passed, going uphill, two four-cylinder yuppies on the Norris Grade outside of Ennis and I began to understand. A woman friend said the truck was "very David" (which irritated me, I think), but was indifferent other than being amused (which irritated me, I'm sure), and men keep trying to buy it.

I am now with the program. I dug out the furry dice I had hung from my first printing press years ago and draped them from the rear-view mirror. I bought a cheap tape deck and play Elmore James singing "Shake Your Money Maker" and other significant rock and roll quite loudly. I roar happily to and fro. I think the jeep runs on testosterone and an astonishing amount of gasoline.

I finally have discovered the secret to enduring male puberty. Shoot Golly.

OTHERS

I was practicng my idle ways the other afternoon and eavesdropping on two people making noises at each other. After some observation I decided I had seen better emotional transactions amongst pieces of furniture. They didn't seem to really be there for each other; each to the other was merely convenient. They came to the encounter—and would remain—empty, vaguely hungry.

Perhaps it is the time of the year. What began as a tide of population on Memorial Day has become a flood by now and many are growing weary treading water. We tend to look through each other when we're tired. Too bad, since looking at—and to—each other would help a lot.

I call it my Berkeleian Theory of Social Dynamics. George Berkeley was a 17th Century bishop of Cloyne (I think) who espoused a narrow philosophical subjectivism that has stuck with us to this day. George is the one who asked: "If a tree falls in the forest and there is no one there to hear it, does the tree exist?" George said no, and I have always been fascinated that we moderns have found this rather selfish view of reality so compelling. If you leave the room, you cease to exist (for me anyway, maybe cease completely), if you come back in, you are there only to service my vision of reality. My goodness, I've always thought that attitude to be very poor manners.

We sat in the cabin and she talked and I listened. Outside, the chickadees were beginning to return to the porch from their summer in the deep forest. I listened to them picnic in the seed and remembered their arrival was my cue to look to the winter-wood gathering.

You listen well, she said. I care about what you have to say, I said. Anything I say? she asked. Yes, I said.

Outside, I had heard that the bull bison had been banging heads all month in the Park, early for them to go into rut, and the junior elk were beginning to squeek across the river. I remembered that this was my cue to enjoy the beginning of the best of seasons.

She said something I admired and I said so. You flatter me, she said. No, I said smiling, that would be a transaction, I would lie sweetly to you for your favor. No, I just admire some things you say, many things you do, you are one of the valuable people, not just to me but to others also.

Outside, the aspen rustled dryly in the wind, going golden from drought and age. I was reminded of the place of the year and looked down at the sunbeams coming through the western window, the few pieces of furniture in the cabin my own Stonehenge after all this time. Yes, that light on that corner of the stove, that angle of light, that length of shadow, means autumn.

Why? she asked. I looked up from the shadows. I have lived an interesting and eclectic life. There have been many opportunities to be wrong and I have often been so. Almost always I was misinformed because I was not listening. Ignorant, hubristic myopia. I wouldn't listen because I thought I was running the show and didn't need to listen. I'm not running the show, I'm just a pilgrim. I listen to you and you tell me more about the show.

Outside, the night things stirred as the shadows stretched flat. The moose in the swale, the small mice coming out and passing the chipmunks in the dry grass on their way to bed. I was reminded to think about the moon, it would be late and cold tonight, pulling the frost behind it.

This place taught me to listen, I said, I could not live well without the reminders it fetches. There is a whole bright world out there that is not me, that I don't control, and if I try to listen well it enlargens and informs my life.

Outside, a bat flapped by the window. Still warm enough for bats. I was reminded to relax, the summer was not over yet.

You are not me, I said. I recognize you as an other and listen to you. It is special to me, this thing you are that is not me.

The corners of her mouth rose. I think you just told me you love me.

I laughed, reminded again of why I do. Yes, I said, you listen well also.

Outside, the wind ran full through the mountains.

GOLD AND HARMONIES

I suppose I am getting a little long in the tooth to be answering the call, but I am compelled—summoned, really—by all the years I wasted not living with elk. Running with the elk is one of my annual religious pilgrimages, and maybe the steps I have lost by tripping over the grey in my beard have been made up for by decaying into a simpleton harmlessness that can be sensed by the great beasts. Maybe they think I'm a shaggy tree. With a limp.

From the hatch-loft small window of my cabin where the cat and I sleep there is an acoustic straight line to the grand meadows across the river in Harriman State Park. Last Monday, the moon flushed like a grouse up out of the trees and the long, whistling wail of the choir rose out in the forest. I turned my head to the window and the cat stirred restless deep in the sleeping bag, knowing my habits, knowing I would be gone soon and he would have to cover the chill of the night alone for a while.

Blood calls to blood. Spiritually transfusable in heat and pulsing harmony. Sometimes in spring I imagine I can feel the sap rising outside, the blood of the plant rising and calling my own. But in autumn, when the elk begin to groan and howl, I know I must go out in the dark, under the moon, and answer the throbbing we all share, we all hear, blood calling to blood.

The spring moon is soft and promising, the summer moon shines. The winter moon glares, but the autumn moon glows and so the path was clear and golden, the aspen shadows like lanterns, the sound of the river a compass and guide. You cannot sneak in the woods this year, things are too dry and the weeds gasp and crack underfoot, so I sauntered to my post, things out in the dark moving away or turning to investigate the stray pilgrim, eyes shining with amused knowledge in the moonlight.

The small waterfall on the western side of the Box Canyon is the last gushing joy of a wandering creek that begins in springs far up the ridge wall of Antelope Valley in Harriman State Park. There are two ancient and regal douglas firs over the springs that harbor eagles and others, and a thick stand of frost-graced aspens that mark the seating just above the stadium of a meadow spreading out to the south, lit bright by the moon. I sat.

To my right, on the western tree line of the clearing, four large bulls paraded before the cows tucked in at the edge of the forest. One cow was close enough that I could see the liquid in her great oval eyes shining as she watched the bulls promenade. One of the smaller bulls—less than half a ton, perhaps—opened its nose and raised its head, the antlers laying flat like great swords on its back, and sang. The doe's eyes glowed fiercely and the other bulls went mad. They tore at the earth and ripped the small trees. They snorted and bellowed and raged. The lead singer charged the bull next to him and the swords clashed and the cows sighed. I stood up. You don't sit down in the presence of legend.

I smelled him before I saw him and I suppose it was the same for him; when the blood boils the sweat goes musk-rank and carries in the frost. I looked over my shoulder around the aspen's silver trunk and saw his head and shoulders shining damply a few feet off, the rest of the great hulk cloaked in golden aspen leaves. He turned and looked at me, eyes swollen and red, the pulse visible in his neck. I knew him, this blood brother, and I suppose it was the same for him. He looked out into the meadow where the cows swayed and the bulls roared, and looked back at me. His nostrils opened and closed heavily, the breath like silver smoke in the moonlight.

"Showtime", I said softly, and he dropped his head to me once, the antlers sparkling, and trotted out into the arena.

Later back at the cabin, I stepped up onto the porch, the moon glowing in the west and the morning birds beginning to stir in the false dawn. I stripped and took the wash basin and poured it over by head, the water steaming and misting in the frost. Up in the loft the cat moved over and I climbed in, the music still calling at the window. I sighed and the blood cooled and the cat purred.

I'm home, I said to him softly.

CUTTING A DEAL

Just the other day I listened while a fellow lied to God. He was in big trouble—as most folks are when they try to cut a deal with God—and he promised that if such-and-such kinds of rescue came about, he would most assuredly do this-and-that. I looked the goon over and decided he didn't have the character to keep a dentist's appointment, much less a bargain with God. I peeked behind his back to see if he had his fingers crossed but he caught me and took offense, so I guffawed off.

Whether your tradition calls God Yaweh or Amithaba or Great Spirit or Higher Guy, it is a commonly held truism that God is omniscient (sees all, hears all) so I never quite got the drift of trying to pull a fast one on Someone with those kinds of connections. Besides, I always had a problem with asking to have the entire pattern of Universal Fate altered for my convenience. It seemed to me that I was plenty lucky to have been born mostly sane and sturdy, and it would be pushing it to ask for much more.

Last May I listened to a guy swear that he would be ready for winter this year (he has lived up here for twenty-hundred years, ran out of wood in March, considered burning the dog and empty bottles, and cut some kind of deal with God that involved his absent-neighbor's wood), and this week we stood in his wood-less yard, in the snow, and I asked him what the penalty was for not keeping a deal with God. He looked blank (he usually does) and I pointed out that God does not work in mysterious ways; God works in perfectly obvious ways. You're going to get cold, I said. The neighbor had gotten wise and not put in any wood this year.

The idea of intervention—cosmic or otherwise—is not a modern notion. Theological literature (Bhadava Gita, Old Testament, Koran, whatever) is full of tales of people cutting a deal to get saved.

Intervening in someone else's life had always seemed slippery stuff to me until a few years ago, when I received instructions from a skunk.

I had left the big wash basin, full of water, outside one autumn day. That night I went out to ogle the moon and found a small skunk swimming in the basin, unable to reach the edge and get out, soaked and short on breath and life. I fished him out and after a half-hearted shake to try to fur up, he lay on the ground panting and soppy. The night had turned cold as a pagan's heart and the little skunk was going to frost over and die before morning, so I took him inside (don't try this at home) and toweled him off in front of the stove and we had a conversation while he dried out.

I apologize, I said, for leaving a death-trap outside. I have found drowned mice and chipmunks in the water bucket before and know that you small ones are peculiar about getting into such things and I should have known better and I'm sorry. Things get into trouble and die in the forest all the time, I said to the skunk while he ate the cat's food, perhaps even I shall some fine day. But I attracted your trouble and am responsible, no excuses. Perhaps you cut a deal with God to get out of the water, perhaps the moon rose so grandly tonight that I needed to come out and see it and you, though I have no idea since I am not in charge of such things.

But I suppose part of the deal we cut with God to be alive is that we do not pass by where help is needed, I said to the skunk while cleaning its ears of some stray parasites. I cannot patrol the forest searching for the helpless because I am not good enough or wise enough to do that, but things that arrive on my porch or in my path seem plain enough, even to me, and it doesn't take that much time to turn aside and offer what I can.

By midnight the little skunk was dry and fed and back out in the yard. I wished him well and thanked him for his help. The moon looked especially glorious and well-placed that night.

BEAUTY RIDES THE BEAST

It began to snow last week in Island Park, an old style big storm, the heavy cloud masses following-folding on one another, crowding into one great continuing snowburst against the highest mountains, a weather pattern as ancient as the mountains themselves. The valley filled quickly with storm, and soon there was another world to change life into, a new bright world to play into, without ever leaving the old place and hearth. I looked out the window at at the knee-wading snow, more still falling, insistently falling with purpose. It is always for me a shock, this chrysallis of the year. 'The universe is rhythmic,' said the old Greeks. The seasons turn one into another. It is very much so here.

Winter is both Beauty and the Beast, and it is here. The serious snow has come, snow to stay. Lots of snow, a foot freshly fallen and more coming, a straight-down snow, layering flakes heaping up in the road and yard, hiding and changing the way we live for the next six months or so. I look out the window at Lesser Frogpond and admire the beauty—the chickadees tumbling like snowflakes in the flocked pines. I go out to fetch wood for the old stove or move the truck about and struggle with the beast. The beast chases folks off the highway and into the ditch, the beast strains convenience by making things cold and deep and difficult. The beauty is easy to look at, but living with her takes some serious thought, takes attending to the chores.

After all these years, it is still an astonishment for me when it comes, the first big snow. I try to get prepared; pile up and tarp down the wood, collect and oil the tools, stash some cash in the sock or Mason jar, get in plenty of new books and mindful hobbies. But I am never prepared emotionally for the change, the sudden snowscape is too large, too dramatic for me to anticipate well, and so my home changes one night and then changes me.

You see, I think the beauty and the beast have finally merged for me. Winter, this most favored of seasons, is so beautiful because it is so difficult, and so there has come a certain comfort in the cold. It once seemed so limiting, so restricting, these miles and months of snow. And winter in the mountains is restrictive of whim, and not very forgiving of carelessness. Now the required alertness has become part of the beauty for me. There have been too many times in the full of summer when the buzzing of the mosquitoes and the afternoon heat on the porch have lulled me into into sloth, the sunshine and the birdsong too much, too rich, and like a man long into the feast, I have nodded at the table. In winter, the chores become part of the feast, and if you do not attend to them, do not pay attention to your small corner of the mountain, you go hungry and cold.

The best days in winter are tidy: the morning care and feeding of the cabin tribe, including the stove. Then the business of the day, done quickly and well, it is hoped. Then finding time and daylight to whisper through the woods on skis or snowshoes, taking inventory of the season, watching the changes, spying out the signs of coming weather and making note of the chores that will require. Where and how is the moon? or the deer? Is the wind fresh and full from the west, or stale and cruel from the north? Then home to the woodpile, just ahead of the storm, putting things close to hand on the porch and re-warming the tiny cabin against the soon dark. There is comfort and beauty being in front of the stove, chores done, on a stormy winter night while the beast prances and howls outside. I have never slept or lived so well as when wrapped in the storm.

And it would not be so beautiful without the beast.

KNOWING HOW

I think I am an affront to the justice of Fate. I am far too clumsy and generally snake-bit to still be alive. I have been variously shot, stabbed, poisoned, run-down, run-over, bitten (by snakes, among others), fallen off of mountains and under oceans, been mauled by accident and by intention, been diseased or stupid beyond hope, and many other mortal catastrophies that are normally considered fatal. I told a friend recently that I figured the only reason I was still around was that God found me amusing.

Just last week I was traipsing along the lava walls of the Box Canyon when my left leg decided to divorce the rest of me and stepped in a scenic crevice, wrenching my knee (again) too far south. I sat down—the knee thing being the human version of a flat tire—and considered amidst the major pain how happy I was. I am, actually, though it is has taken a few years to know that.

Every person I have ever known who is past the age of consent and consumed of good cheer has had to learn how to be happy. I remember being nine years old and quite happy, but that is the kind of happiness that is often handed to you then; a combination of being merely nine and still mostly innocent and ignorant. Later we learn that troubles are also often handed to you, and things take on a greater weight as the miles and years pile up. A lot of the problem is that things that are handed to you are hard to possess and take responsibility for. In the same manner we learn to deny that last week's hideous incident was any of our doing, it follows that happiness must also be an accident, not our responsibility, none of our own doing. It's a kind of siege mentality that doesn't leave much room for joy.

Then there are the three 'R's of later life: Regret, Resentment, and Remorse. Personally, I remorse plenty and often. But resentment is becoming a stranger. I pulled the bandana from around my neck and wrapped up the lame knee. I regret the knee but I don't resent the poor thing; I have dragged it into many risky places and it has almost always helped me out of danger. I grumbled up and stiff-legged it down the trail. Coming around a large old Doug fir I came into near-contact with a moose so pretty it dazzled my eyeballs and lifted my lips over the teeth. Cosmic compensation for the fall, I suppose. I am responsible for the knee injury but I am also responsible for harming it in a place with such good-looking moose. No resentment required.

Learning how to be happy is like learning any other skill: figure out what it is you want to make or do, get together the tools and things you need, and practice a lot. I heard a local wag the other day saying money couldn't buy happiness but it could buy living well, and doing that could make him happy. I'd heard that before, but tools like money seem to be out of the question for someone with my lifestyle and destiny, so a few years ago I proposed to discover what living well (for me) was, and how to get there without paying for it in cash.

At the time I decided this it was 45° below outside, with a ripe north wind, and the cat and I were huddled inside the thin cabin in front of the pesky stove on a platform of books, since the thinner carpet had been given over to frost. We were out of coffee, almost out of water, the pipe tobacco was as meager as the pantry, the storm had been howling for two days and seemed to be just getting warmed up, the roads were blown shut in three states, three days before I had one of those little escapades where I fell face first off a mountain with the skis trailing behind, my body being rearranged in painful ways, and I think the cat had worms.

There being little else to do, I pulled the blanket closer and pondered happiness. The books we nested on were good ones, books you like to read again and will. The inexpensive prints icing up on the walls were of good taste and required being looked at often and in different lights. The wind coming in through the cracks in the walls smelled fresh and clean. I decided it was a nice day, a nicer day than I had enjoyed in many other places—and I have been many other places. As I got up to break up the last piece of furniture for stove wood, I decided that I liked it here because I had chosen to be here, and be here this way. It wasn't handed to me. At this mid-point in life I had decided to take responsibility, finally, for where and how I am. As the pot on the stove scorched the snow I was trying to melt for dried wildflower-weed tea, I looked around and noticed I was living well; no question about it, I knew how to live well.

I got up and looked out the window as best I could and grinned about knowing how. As the snow swallowed the last of the truck, I knew I had arrived at living well and being happy.

About the Author

David Hays lives at Lesser Frog-pond in Last Chance, Idaho, five miles from the continental divide and twenty miles west of Yellowstone National Park. He came to the Rocky Mountains after three years in China, spent as a Buddhist monk and Barefoot Doctor. He has worked as a teacher, journalist, and Mississippi riverboat banjo player. He received a Ph.D. in cultural anthropology from the University of California at San Diego.

Photo by Robert Bower